HOW TO MAKE MONEY ONLINE NOW

21 ideas to work and earn money from wherever you want with Trading Bitcoin and Forex, Blogger, Web Development, Creating Animation Video

DIEGO DE GIOVANNI

blame be held against the publisher for any reparation, damages, or monetary loss due to the information herein, either directly or indirectly.

Respective authors own all copyrights not held by the publisher.

The information herein is offered for informational purposes solely, and is universal as so. The presentation of the information is without contract or any type of guarantee assurance.

The trademarks that are used are without any consent, and the publication of the trademark is without permission or backing by the trademark owner.

All trademarks and brands within this book are for clarifying purposes only and are the owned by the owners themselves, not affiliated with this document.

TABLE OF CONTENTS

INTRODUCTION

I might initially want to thank you for setting aside the effort to peruse this instructional kindle book – you won't be disillusioned. This digital book has been composed for individuals wherever to exploit and has not been composed for others to benefit from. So, if you don't mind don't hesitate to impart it to loved ones, however kindly don't sell it onto others.

Regardless you are a busy mother, a stay at home father, a college student, or just want to earn some extra money with your spare time – doing some extra work can help you make some nice money from home.

A quick internet research can reveal many to do work from home scams. They charge you upfront high fees and lure you to work with them.

"But actually, they are just cheating you out of your hard-earned money".

What you should already have (as a minimum)

This is not rocket science and it's quite self-explanatory, but it's worth saying nevertheless. To be able to utilize these methods, you will need the following:

1. Computer or Laptop

2. An internet connection

3. Bank account

3. Spare Time

Who would benefit from this?

Everyone! Whether you're a stay at home parent or you work from home, or you are a student – many of these proven methods are a great way to earn some extra cash and will help you to save some money

1 EARN MONEY FROM SKILLS

✴ 3 Different Way to Earn quick money from home.

There are many ways to earn money online, but we are going to highlight 3 Major Categories from which you can find the best way to earn money from home

1: Required Skills to do some Jobs/Projects.

2: Simple To do Tasks / Virtual Assistance.

3: Invest and Earn Profits

So, to be honest, these are the Major Ways to Earn money but hey wait let me elaborate you the sub ways under these categories from which you can really pick the best skill to work on ant get yourself ready for the opportunities that might come near soon and knock your luck door.

✴ Required Skills to do some Jobs/Projects.

✴ Graphics Design
I bet you've been there:

Sitting at a customer's concise, understanding that the plan you're going to do is dull and needs validness. Be that as it may, if that is the thing that the customer needs... you should set your desire aside and adhere to the guidelines.

Here's the thing !!!

Continually following the guidelines doesn't help on the off chance that you need to demonstrate your innovative side, adapt new methods and fabricate a stand-apart portfolio. It doesn't give you much opportunity and space for experimentation. For imaginative craftsmen, that is torment!

The uplifting news is:

To profit as a visual creator, you don't generally need to tail another person's vision. There are a lot of easy revenue openings that would enable you to plan what you need, the manner to create and abstract ideas from yours own,

Here are some skills on which you can work on and grow into your creativity

- comics and graphic novels

- coloring books

- web icons and custom illustrations

- fonts

- social media images and icon packs

- emojis and stickers

- printable wall art

Logo Design

Logo designing is used to specify a brand or an organization name. Today's business strategy has changed in more amount than before. To get maximum benefits, we must have to establish our presence online. And to create our existence on the Internet of People, to establish our Vision or a brand "Our Company's Logo" is most essential.

So this necessity could become your job opportunity, if you have talent, have a creative mind and have a skill on designing software like adobe Photoshop then you are most eligible person to earn massive income online.

Actually logo designing is most critical issue. If you managed it properly then success is yours!

Here are some tips to Create Logo Design, the steps you need to follow are as follows:-

Before going through these tips you should aware from how to use Photoshop.

•First you can create a rough design on a paper if you are full-fledged with your drawing skills or you can start creating on Photoshop.

•In Photoshop you need to work on document for which you need to take a custom size paper of width 5 inches, height 5 inches and resolution of 300 pixels.

•You can either take RGB mode or CMYK as it both will function accordingly but to view a clear image CMYK is considered to be better as RGB creates pixels and gets blur if you zoom your image.

•To create a logo you can make the use of pen tool or you can take brush tool but pen tool creates better sharp design. For pen tool you have to work on path and a layer in which you can start creating design.

•You must see to it that every design you have created, has its own layer and path. If correction needed you can select its path and by clicking Alt button you can work accordingly to it.

•After creating design in your path it will ask you for selecting and then you need to right click on path and say make selection to add color to it.

•You can also increase the size by CTRL+T. Also you can create a duplicate layer if you need the same design but you need to flip it by right clicking and say Flip horizontal or vertical you can make use of other options too i.e. Scale, Rotate, Skew, Perspective, Warp etc.

•If you want to add on some effects to your logo you can make use of blending options and accordingly make use of it usually we apply "Stroke Option" to it.

•You can also make use of Hue/Saturation, Color balance, brightness/contrast to make color changes. This option you will find in Photoshop software (Image -> Adjustments.)

•After all these steps followed you have to save the file in PSD and JPEG format and if changes required you can accordingly work on PSD file.

Adobe Photoshop Skills

•Adobe Photoshop is another trending tool where you can work on some photo editing work and earn some good amount form it, So the solution is you need to join the Adobe Photoshop Online Course. To choose the best online selling course you have to research little about high demanding skills. What are the highest demanding and highest paid graphics designing skills out there? Once you spend some money on learning graphics designing or adobe photoshop expert skills, it will make you responsible to get the return within profit. and for that, you must need to pay for the adobe photoshop course. And it's your investment.

•Once you spend some money on learning graphics designing or adobe photoshop expert skills, it will make you responsible and serious to get a return within profit. There are two advantages of online adobe photoshop course to earn money is that you will get complete details and premium stuff about the course before you join. 2nd you will get the knowledge about professional adobe photoshop skills.

•The second method is to join any offline course out there on Udemy or YouTube. Find out the top-quality people and institution in your city known as an expert in adobe photoshop. At the same time at home, you should use your time watching adobe photoshop tutorials and practicing on all those on you spare time.

•Now you got the lessons on how to use and design and edit your imagination power in Adobe Photoshop. But it's not finished yet, it's a start. So to become expert practice more and more until you really become an "Expert". Practice will increase your speed to complete the designing and editing tasks in a very quick pace of time. It will increase the accuracy and identify creativity, and perfection into your work.

T-Shirt Design

A T-shirt design that works out in color, text, slogan or some promotion about any product etc., is the one that people want to buy. The design must be Attractive with a unique idea. It requires a careful selection of some elements such as colors and text etc.

After you brainstorm and designed a brilliant T-shirt, you have to acquire some marketing skills to sell your work. Knowing some marketing selling strategies is critical if you are a getting started with freelance designer Career. There is some potential for the growth of your small T-shirt selling brand, you have to market it well. So, both the designing and marketing aspects should be handled properly into. If you do that, your chances for the growth of your brand would be higher.

Some people who consider t-shirt designing as a hobby & make millions of dollars. You can also sell your creative T-shirt design and sell them successfully with Good marketing skills

✴ Here Is how you can Sell T-Shirt Designs Online

01. Work on Unique T-Shirt Design Idea

The initial step to take for selling T-shirt plans is to have an incredible structure thought. Without an exceptional thought, it will be progressively hard to persuade customers or clients to purchase the shirts. All things considered, they are purchasing the structure and not the T-shirt.

What it means is that T-shirt as clothing are bounty in business sectors. They can buy any of these easygoing wears. Along these lines, they are probably going to settle on the T-shirt that has an awesome structure on it.

In this way, make it sure that your T-shirt plan thought is remarkable and appealing. It must discover the generally faltering consideration of individuals immediately from the start. That is the way to sell the shirts. Without any such thought, don't consider becoming wildly successful in the business department.

02. Brainstorming

The most ideal approach to get a shirt structure thought is to conceptualize. Plunk down with your group to discover which thought will sell. You have numerous alternatives. You can make sharp quips, charming plans, or have roar with laughter jokes that everyone adores. Individuals like to wear such T-shirts.

Another choice is to simply investigate the thoughts in regards to films and prevalent TV serials, without infringing their copyrights. You can likewise misuse some social side of individuals. Ensure that you have an extraordinary plan thought when you sell your craft structure to the intended interest group.

03. Learn To Design

In case you are not a designer and still want to sell T-shirt designs as your business, you should acquire some working knowledge of designs. Learn about typography and colors and how to make a good choice. Learn also how to use Adobe Photoshop. This software will help you create graphics easily.

You can also have a good experience of using clipart and word shapes. It will be useful in enhancing your image on the shirts. Also, use new apps like Word swag and Over to have some mastery over design. Get some design tips as well from online experts.

If designing is not your forte, hire a freelance graphic designer to do the job for you. In that case, you can then focus on increasing your sales.

Either you design it yourself as a freelancer, or hire a designer, make it doubly sure that the design is unique. Every element of fonts, words, clipart, images, etc. should make an impression.

04. Here Are Some Of The Printing And Selling Sites

• Merch By Amazon

Merchandise by Amazon is an extraordinary stage to sell your T-shirt plans on the web. One of the upsides of this site is its high traffic volume. As indicated by a gauge, Amazon gets around 669 million guests for each month.

This far more noteworthy than joined traffic gotten by numerous different destinations, for example, Teespring, Zazzle, CafePress, and so forth. In this way, gain admittance to those a large number of individuals a large number of whom you can transform into clients of your custom shirt.

You will get extra selling assets apparatuses at Amazon. You can utilize these apparatuses to dissect your traffic to have an understanding into dealing with the business appropriately.

• CafePress And Zazzle

Both these locales are prevalent for their simplicity of information exchange and item arrangement. These locales set the cost of printing your T-shirt plan. They likewise let you pick your sovereignty which is added to the shirt's base cost.

At Zazzle and CafePress the base costs are appealing. They likewise give you an exhibition reward. You can likewise get to a shirt creator apparatus to make your own plan before selling it from these destinations.

• Redbubble

With Redbubble, you can set up your store to sell the printed T-shirts. The site will choose the base cost. In any case, you are permitted to decide your markup.

• Shopify

Simply set up a shop at Shopify and you have fast access to a printer just as a drop shipper. You would then be able to deal with the correct harmony between your cost and different choices.

Truth be told, there are numerous other extraordinary shirts printing locales, for example, Custom Ink, Spreadshirt, Teespring, Printful, Vistaprint, UberPrints, and Print Aura. Contrast these locales with discover which one enables you to set your costs higher, other than printing your shirts on schedule. Most such destinations will likewise give you shirt producer instrument to structure the clothing without anyone else.

05. Make a Marketing Strategy

After you have a shocking structure thought and opened a retail facade or made a site to sell the plan, it is currently an opportunity to advertise it. Indeed, advertising is a pivotal stage. It can represent the moment of truth your business. Showcasing

is tied in with concocting novel approaches to contact the intended interest group. It needs a sound methodology.

Since you mean to sell T-shirt structures on the web, it naturally brings the SEO best practices to mind. Site design improvement is tied in with expediting your retail facade or site the top list items. At the point when potential clients type catchphrases identified with your business, your site must be obvious on the top indexed lists that you can guarantee by the correct enhancement procedures.

Showcasing likewise implies that you have to make sense of your objective client. Who is the one that is well on the way to purchase your T-shirt? You make a structure. Be that as it may, which age-gathering and social or instructive foundations your clients originate from?

Discover your optimal client and afterward make an arrangement to sell your T-shirt to that crowd. Try not to attempt to offer to everybody.

You will likewise be searching for influencers who can discuss your T-shirt plans on the web. They can enable you to help your business hugely. This is on the grounds that they have a huge number of supporters who will come to think about your business. Influencer showcasing is likewise an extraordinary method to assemble your image personality.

At that point, you ought to likewise investigate the advertising openings via web-based networking media. Open records on various social channels like Facebook and Twitter. At that point, normally post your substance about your one of a kind T-shirts to draw in purchasers.

These are the key focuses to consider while selling T-shirt structures on the web. Deal with every one of the angles well by contributing your time and cash cautiously.

✳ Make Money From Web Development

This is also another best approach to build your skills first and then make some sample websites to test your skills and show them to random people for feedback, if people really like your Web development work then you are good to go with this skill,

But your question how to make out from it? Well now we will discuss all about web development and how you can make a website and earn money from it!

Step:1 How to build a portfolio like a professional?

You have to have a site and a point of arrival. On the off chance that you are in the web planning industry, you should realize what I'm trying to say.

You should be obvious to the general population. You should be known and permit to be come to on any stage, whenever of the day.

The way toward making a site is simple. What's next is intense!

You have to have a straightforward web composition that feature what your identity is and what's in for the potential customer.

Regarding proportion, you should share 10% of the substance on 'about you' and the equalization 90% about the customer. You know, the reasons why they have to try and take a gander at your profile.

Step 2: Using the right tools for web design

How to begin website architecture as a tenderfoot? The stunt is by utilizing the correct instruments.

A website specialist regularly have a wide scope of devices available to them however in the event that you are a finished learner (imagining that web planning can win you cash), at that point you just need a couple of devices to begin.

Those tools are:

⟩ Turnkey and expert subjects

⟩ Page manufacturer

⟩ Web facilitating

Indeed, you just need the over three to begin with website specialist as a novice.

Select the right professional themes

This is very mission-critical. You need to have a wide range of good themes to help you kick-start some of your web design gigs.

Choosing the right themes is very important when is comes to building a good career because it will either turn on or turn off your potential clients. So, make sure you are mindful of this.

When it comes to the professional WordPress themes, for developing I recommend you to start small — this means that while it is always good to have at least 50 custom themes in your toolbox, you can start with a small figure (anywhere between 5 to 10).
These professional themes must be easy to configure, and it is almost an important requirement to have a drag and drop feature.

"You don't have much coding skill, remember?"

Why is it important to choose the right themes?

For starters, it needs to be easy to use because you have limited skills as a fresh web designer. More importantly, you don't need to get your hands dirty with the coding and all those mind bogging stuffs.

Secondly, the license would need to allow you to use it without limit (unlimited usage). You wouldn't want to buy a theme each time when you get a new client because it is going to eat away your earnings very quick.

Make Yourself Available Every time

Your customers need to realize that you exist. On the off chance that potential customers don't have any acquaintance with you exist, your work will be somewhat harder. Chances are; however, you are associated with a bigger number of individuals than you might suspect. It's essential to begin with those individuals and let them realize that you are currently accessible to construct sites.

I made my accessibility known on my own site if you mean to assemble sites for other people, you do need to have your own). I messaged people I'd done work for previously and let them realize I was accessible once more. I augmented my current systems administration associations, and, out of that, I started to arrange the initial couple of tasks.

If you haven't had any experience building sites, that is alright. We need to begin some place and I can't think about a superior time than the present moment. Figure out how to get your first web advancement customer.

Use the Right Platform

To make solid $5000+ a month as a part-time, you're going to need to be very quick and fast. If you don't really know how to build websites from scratch, now isn't the time to learn. If you *do* know how to build websites from scratch, I highly recommend that you set that knowledge aside for now. You need to use a platform.

WordPress is my favorite and I recommend it highly. It has a proven track record, open source development team behind it, community support, diverse theme options, and momentum.

Go out buy any books on web development (yet), enroll in any classes at your local college (it's a fast class and someone passionate is teaching it). You need to focus on getting results as efficiently and as effectively as possible. There has never been a better time than right now to make use of a platform that's already been built, and is well past the tipping point of quality and popularity.

If there are particular tasks that are not a part of your core strengths, consider finding a freelancer to help you with those and get yourself more polished for the competition in web development.

Charge the Right Price

If you're going to make Solid $5000+ per month, you can not be building websites for only a few hundred dollars. You're doing yourself and your clients a disservice. You need to have a open mind and charge a fair price. Consider the value that you're able to provide by leveraging a platform and by helping them put that platform to use.

If you're going to make $5000+ a month, you can't be building websites for only a few bucks,

Wrap your mind around the value time and focus on what building a website can do for your client's business. I recommend you charge $2500 per project. Don't go for less than $1000 on per project and make sure that you can finish the project with an average of over $75/hour or before deadline (that's what it takes to make $5000+ a month working part-time).

Master Your Skill Craft

As you begin to develop a traction and good experience, it's very important to invest in your time, value, education and focus on mastering your skill craft. Now is the time to start reading books and blogs on web development. Enroll in some premium online courses. Pick an area or specific skill to specialize and begin to focus on developing your skill set further into that area.

Attend events in your area of interest and network with others strong people. Ask the right questions and learn from the experience of those who've gone before you into those skills. As the demand for websites grows, so will the number of people trying to meet that demand. If you are going to stand out, you need to constantly work towards a mastery of what you do and what you work for.

As your success allows you time to sit back, go ahead and enjoy a short rest, then get right back to it and work continually towards mastery of your skills.

★ Build a Mobile App That Actually Makes Money

Why do you want to build an app?

Mobile applications are a great way for business owners to make improvements to their company. They are also the perfect platform if you think that your idea will be the next big hit, like Instagram or Snapchat. Regardless of your reason for creating an app, I'm sure you have something in common with other prospective developers. All of you want to make money. First of all, I commend you for doing the research before you get started building your first app. I've seen so many people who were naive enough to think that just because they created an app, it would automatically generate money. That's not true. Here's an analogy. If you start a new business, will it automatically make money? Absolutely not .Fortunately, you've come to the right place. As an expert in the mobile application industry, I have the knowledge and experience to help steer you in the right direction. 90% of time spent on mobile devices is in apps. Build a profitable mobile app in less time and at a lower cost than traditional solutions with Build Fire Consumers clearly love to use apps, so the opportunity is there. The key is finding out how to choose the perfect app that will peak user interest and ultimately get downloads. But you need to realize that downloads alone don't always directly translate to dollars. Building an app is expensive, and you'll come across hidden development costs along the way. So before you dump all of your money into your new idea, you've got to make sure it will generate a profit.

Here's what you need to know.

Purchasing something in-app vs a mobile site

For those of you who already have an existing business, I'm going to assume that your company has a website. Hopefully (for your sake) that site has been optimized for mobile devices. Websites that aren't mobile friendly will turn visitors away, so if that's not something you've done, it needs to be a priority.

Now, let's discuss the customer experience and how it relates to their purchasing habits. Do you think users prefer buying on a mobile site or directly through a mobile application?

Apps wins. Here's why.

Convenience was the number one answer from respondents.

The other top responses also mirror convenience and enhance user satisfaction.

Your customers want everything fast. As I said earlier, if your website isn't optimized for mobile devices, speed can be an issue. But that's not a problem when people navigate through your app. Think of your app like any other business. The easiest way to make money is by keeping the customers happy and keep them coming back. In addition to speed and convenience, the checkout process on a mobile purchase is also much simpler. Purchases on an app get charged directly to the customer's credit card associated with their Google Play or App Store account.

Look how easy it is to buy something within an app if your customers have Apple Pay linked to their devices.

One click and done. It's that easy for the customer and you start getting money instantly. How does this compare to a mobile site? We've already established that speed is a factor, but for argument's sake, let's say your mobile site already runs fast too. What else could slow the customer down? They won't have their cards or accounts linked to your mobile site, so they'll have to input all of their information. The customer has to log in to their PayPal account or enter their credit card information. Overall, it's just a longer process and more of a headache for the user. Plus, typing out all of that information on a small screen leaves room for errors that can slow things down even more. Don't get me wrong. I'm not saying your mobile site shouldn't have a checkout page or have ways to generate money through credit card purchases. All I'm trying to do is emphasize that *in-app purchases are better.*

The platform that you launch your app on matters too. Take a look at the difference between the iOS and Android purchases.

The average purchase per user on iOS platforms are more than double Android's.

That doesn't mean that you should choose one over another. While iOS may have a higher number for the average purchase, Android dominates in terms of total users. Looking back at fourth-quarter smartphone sales last year, there were 432 million devices sold. Of the

432 million phones, 77 million had iOS software while 352 million ran on Android's platform. The two platforms combined for 99% of the market share, but Android alone accounts for 81.7%.With that said, 16% of Android developers earn over $5,000 per month with their mobile apps, and 25% of iOS developers make over $5,000 through app earnings. So keep these figures in mind if you're only planning to release on just one operating system.

What if you are selling physical products?

We briefly touched on this earlier, but I wanted to continue to elaborate on this topic. To successfully sell products through an app, you've got to put yourself in the minds of a mobile shopper.

40% of mobile users have bought something online with their smartphone.
This number continues to grow each year.
There are generational trends too. For example, Millennials dominate this category.
63% of Millennials have used smartphones and tablets to make a purchase.
I'm going to show you an example of a company that knows how to use their mobile app to drive sales and make money. You can follow their lead and apply their strategies to your app if you're selling a physical product as well. I'm referring to the company, Touch of Modern. 70% of the company's total sales are generated from mobile devices. Roughly two-thirds of those sales come directly from their app. So how do they do it Roughly 150,000 to 200,000 users download this app each month.57% of their shoppers are repeat customers. When you have the ability to focus on customer acquisition and customer retention at

the same time, it's a formula for success. It's their checkout flow that makes Touch of Modern so successful.

When you download the app, you'll create a profile that securely saves your information That way whenever customers open the app, they can get straight to shopping.

Here's how it looks.

It's a simple navigation screen. Customers can easily search for and scroll through items that they're interested in. Once they find something that peaks their interest, they can click on the product to find out more information. C Now the user will see a detailed description of the product in addition to a larger photo. If they like what they see and read, they can add it to their shopping cart with just one click.

Once it's in their cart, the customer can checkout in just one simple click.

That's it. Their app allows users to complete the shopping and purchase process in just three steps. There's way less friction here compared to a mobile ecommerce site. Plus, Touch of Modern can communicate with their customers better from the mobile app. They send app users notifications with daily deals and discounted items to encourage more purchases. Ultimately, this strategy works. If you're currently selling products on your website and mobile site, you can generate more revenue by successfully building a mobile app.

Build a profitable mobile app in less time and at a lower cost than traditional solutions with Build Fire

Free apps vs paid apps

Something else you'll want to consider is whether you're going to charge users to download your app. On average,

you would obviously generate a higher revenue per download. It may seem like a nice way to get some up-front profits, but you might turn people away if they have to pay. 90% of the apps on the Apple App Store are free. But that doesn't mean you have to go that route. Paid apps are a great way to get more loyal customers. If they are willing to make the initial purchase just for installation, they may be more likely to use it and make additional purchases. However, if you're an established brand that already has retail channels and existing customers (like Touch of Modern), it's probably in your best interest to offer your app for free. People download those apps so they can save money and receive discounts, not spend more money just to have the option of shopping.
Keep in mind; your app will also have competition.
So customers realize that they can find something similar and potentially better for free, rather than paying to download yours.

With free apps, you may get significantly more downloads, but the users could be less engaged. If they don't pay, there's no commitment. They could potentially download your app, check it out once and never use it again. While they may sound discouraging, you shouldn't look at it that way. It doesn't cost you anything to have users download your app and never use it. Sure, you'd prefer active users, but at the end of the day, it's not going to be detrimental to your company.
If you're on the fence about releasing a free or paid app, I'd lean towards recommending a free download. It will increase the chances of getting more downloads, and you can make money through other sources.
Here's a look at some global averages based on the CPM for different mobile app advertisements.

So there's definitely some money to be made here if you can sell advertising space on your app. Keep in mind, these numbers are just averages, and they aren't set in stone. If you have tons of active daily users and your app grows in popularity, you can negotiate a higher rate from advertisers based on those numbers.

Another way to generate money from a free app is with upgrades and subscriptions. Users can download the app for free and use the basic functions.

Then you can offer premium content or functions based on a monthly subscription.

Let's look at how a popular dating app accomplishes this on their platform.

I'm sure you've heard of Tinder. The concept is super simple. Users create a profile and add photos of themselves. Based on their location and preferences, they'll see photos of other users who match their search criteria (age, gender, etc.).

If they like another user's profile, they swipe right. If they don't, they swipe left.

When two people both swipe right on each other, they get connected and can start a conversation. Everyone who downloads this app has access to these features for free. But there are certain restrictions. If users swipe right on too many profiles in a day, they can't continue searching for 24 hours.

That's where a premium subscription comes in play. If users want to have unlimited likes, they can upgrade their account. The upgraded subscription comes with other bonus features like a location change, rewinds, and an experience without advertisements. You can apply this same business model to your app to make money. Let users download and use the app for free, but withhold the best features for users who are willing to pay.

Conclusion

Not all apps make money. If your plan is to just build one without a strategy and just sit back to collect your money, you'll be in for a rude awakening. Like a business, you need to have a strategy and goal before you start building an app. Mobile user prefer apps compared to mobile sites. So while your company definitely needs a website that's optimized for mobile devices, an app can make the customer experience much better. Sure, you'll have some upfront costs when you build, develop, and launch your app. But you can save time and money by creating an app through the Build Fire platform. If you're selling a physical product, having a mobile app will help you generate more money.

✴ Earn Money from Video and Animation

Make Money Editing Videos: 5 Websites that Pay

Video editing is the arrangement and manipulation of video shots. Simply put its an artistic and technical skill that requires adding special effects, structuring and more to videos. In this guide we will be sharing 5 websites where you can make money editing videos. The video industry nowadays is booming, with more and more people requiring professional help to create quality video content. So if you are already good at this then hold on, we have something big for you this time!

Being a freelance video editor can be demanding but equally rewarding. And even if you aren't a professional, just by having the right video editing software and some skill set you can start earning good money.

Video editing is the course of action and control of video shots. Just put its a masterful and specialized aptitude that requires including enhancements, organizing and more to recordings. In this guide we will share 5 sites where you can profit editing recordings. The video business these days is blasting, with an ever increasing number of individuals requiring proficient assistance to make quality video content. So on the off chance that you are as of now great at this, at that point hang tight, we have something important for you this time!

Being an independent video editorial manager can be requesting yet similarly fulfilling. What's more, regardless of whether you aren't an expert, just by having the correct video editing programming and some range of abilities you can begin winning great cash.

Websites that pay you for Video Editing Skills:

Viedit is an extraordinary stage for independent video editors. This stage enlists a wide range of editors, artists, and videographers. Consultants can make business recordings, internet-based life cuts, home recordings, travel films and that's only the tip of the iceberg. At whatever point a customer posts an undertaking, specialists can see these ventures and send recommendations with their own proposed cost for it. When the customer acknowledges your proposition, they pay the concurred measure of cash to ViEdit. When the video is finished and acknowledged, Viedit will discharge the installment.

As VidEdit has consultants and customers from 100 unique nations, the organization pays its specialists through generally all installment mediums e.g **PayPal, Bank Transfer, Credit** Card and the sky is the limit from there. The organization charges an expense of 5-15% from the complete installment to the consultant, contingent upon the sort of video mentioned.

MOFILM is a UK based substance maker organization. The organization makes video content for different organizations and brands. Video editors from everywhere throughout the world can pitch video thoughts or make recordings trying to win cash from intrigued brands.

On the off chance that you want to contend with the best, at that point register yourself on their site. On the off chance that you fit the necessities for a undertaking, an organization delegate will connect with you.

The organization pays its consultants through Bank move. The installment sum will fluctuate from venture to extend, so there's no standard charge to it. The organization will pay the consultant half of the sum forthright and the other half will be paid once the alters are finished.

1.Uscreen

Uscreen is a video on interest (VOD) stage and a specialist co-op that empowers people and organizations to sell recordings on the web. So on the off chance that you are a videographer or proofreader, the organization encourages you make your very own video selling stage. You can sell singular recordings or offer paid memberships. Through this stage, you can sell your recordings at any value you want, you will be the proprietor of your own store.

Uscreen has various installment choices you can get installment from your clients. These installment doors incorporate, PayPal, Stripe and Braintree. As a byproduct of facilitating you video store, Uscreen charges a little expense for every month, going from $99-388 relying upon the quantity of supporters you need for your recordings.

2.Tongal

Tongal is another incredible video content creation stage committed to making recordings for a wide range of computerized stages. They enlist a wide range of scholars, illustrators, videographers and editors. The organization capacities as rivalry site, where a video venture is posted with the prize subtleties. The consultants would then be able to pitch their thoughts through storyboarding and so on. When chosen for your pitch, the film cause will to get financing for the video. When the last alters are done, you will get paid by the organization.

Tongal pays its victors through four installment portals including, PayPal, Direct Deposit, Wire Transfer and Check. The prize cash will change from undertaking to extend so there is no standard sum that is paid.

✶ Create Your Video Content

1. Upload Your Videos To YouTube

This is presumably the most widely recognized way that most video business visionaries start to begin profiting with recordings. It's drop-dead easy to do and doesn't require a huge interest in video gear to begin:

1.   Create a channel on YouTube

2.   Start transferring recordings to your channel routinely.

When you begin to gather watchers and you begin to construct the quantity of supporters of your channel, you can join to adapt your recordings by permitting YouTube to show promotions on your recordings. The more perspectives your recordings get, the more cash that you will procure from the individuals who view or snap on your video promotions. You can begin a YouTube channel today however profit will take an extended period of time to work after some time except if you figure out how to strike gold and make a viral video immediately. There are different approaches to profit with your YouTube channel too, however, which we detail in different articles here on Video Entrepreneur Magazine:

2. Produce Videos or Offer A Video Related Service to Others

There are numerous individuals that need to begin profiting with recordings, however they are unequipped for making proficient quality recordings for themselves. You can assist these individuals with creating top notch recordings for their venture on an independent premise. Along these lines, you can acknowledge their requests to make, alter or even market recordings and get paid for the administrations that you give them. Obviously, you can likewise offer your video generation administration locally for extraordinary occasions, for example, weddings and business gatherings.

3. Make Video Lessons

In the event that you are a topic master in a specific specialty or point, it's a good thought for you to begin making preparing recordings identified with your specialty. Step by step instructions to and instructional exercise recordings, help your group of spectators adapt more data about a subject they are keen on, just as to take care of their issues. For example, on the off chance that you are a health specialist, you can make video exercises about how to do activities to get in shape, how to do activities to pick up muscle, how to do certain activities effectively, and so on.

You can offer your recordings by means of a membership administration, where your customers pay a month to month or yearly expense for proceeded with access to your recordings, you can offer them online on a compensation for each view premise or you can sell your recordings as a pack by means of download or by sending them on plate or other memory stockpiling gadget. You can conceivably profit with recordings beginning today by making and selling instructional exercise recordings.

4. Sell Your Stock Footage

Like stock photographs, there are likewise online administrations that sell stock film for business use. These stock recordings and "b-move" cuts are generally utilized by business video makers to finish their tasks. On the off chance that you can make proficient recordings of fascinating subjects, you can begin selling your stock film through those sites and profit with recordings immediately. Remember that on the off chance that you sell stock film through these sites you will part income of all offers of your recordings the specialist organization that has your stock film; they have the video, handle the exchanges and market their site. In the event that your recordings have a specific subject or center, as submerged video film, for instance, you can likewise sell stock film straightforwardly through your very own site. In the event that you have an enormous enough reach, you could conceivably begin making with your recordings rapidly, yet for most video business visionaries it will require a long time to manufacture a gainful market.

5. Subsidiary Advertising and Selling Product Placement on Viral Videos

Another approach to profit with recordings is to make or secure the rights to viral recordings and afterward sell item position or subsidiary items through those recordings. Viral recordings are short pieces that individuals will appreciate watching and sharing. You can make motivating, interesting, questionable or passionate recordings and offer them by means of your internet based life records trusting that your social associations will remark and share your recordings among their companions and that they will impart them to their companions, as well – however that is the most difficult way; there's no assurance a video will circulate around the web and you may make one hundred of them before viewing a video get on and spread quickly.

Hanging around or while going around the nation means going with friends to some party night. An incredible workstation that is stacked with altering programming, hard drive of film, and a respectable pair of earphones is extremely all you need. Having a work area with additional screens, full keyboard mouse, monster speakers, USB center points and all that are incredible, however unnecessary.

For what apparatus you do require,

10 years prior, not too bad quality video configurations were all the while being caught onto tape and other proprietary frameworks, requiring control decks and catch cards that were more costly than my truck. Nowadays I'm ready to alter for offices who value the all-computerized work process as much as I do. Without a doubt, they at times shoot on DSLRs, however I consistently get film shot on BMCCs, mid to top of the line Sony frameworks, Canon C-Series, and the sky is the limit from there. All media winds up on a hard drive which is simpler for them, and keeps it simple (and modest!) for me.

Have an inclination that binge spending? Alright, here's a rundown of things that I utilize day by day in my home office. It makes the experience more pleasant and bit increasingly proficient, so I've developed this after some time.

*Macintosh Macbook Pro with maximized RAM and an OWC
SSD Startup Disk*

Sony MDR 7506 Headphones

USB Hub

DisplayPort to VGA Adapter (for outer screen 1)

Precious stone USB to VGA Adapter (for outer screen 2)

OWC Mercury Elite Pro Mini External Hard Drives

Logitech MediaPlay Wireless Mouse

In the event that you don't have a work process or
customers nailed down, start by altering a couple of basic
activities for individuals you have worked with before. Do
an in the background alter, or volunteer to do a promotion
or something to that affect for them. (Reward tip: Do it
for somebody who has a huge online life following so it
gets a ton of additional traffic, and potential referrals!)
Editing a couple of spec activities will cause you to
experience every one of the paces in question, and you'll
begin to refine your work process while building your
altering portfolio. Which leads me to the self-evident…

**Have a strong altering reel or instances of work, on
the web and prepared to appear**

When requesting for work, you'll have to give verification
of aptitude. Either a few decent, short alters you've taken a
shot at, or an assemblage reel of segments of various
altering ventures. It has a couple of various completed
video alters to flaunt, however try to send the alter that will

be most similar to what your potential customer is needing you to accomplish for them.

Get your stockpiling within proper limits

After my initial couple of employments, I understood that I needed nearby stockpiling for my media and my reinforcements, however I needed to reinforcement customer drives too. That is to say, consider the possibility that when I dispatched the drive back the Fedex bundle was lost or harmed. I chose to become tied up with a capacity framework that addressed my issues, and I've been utilizing these drives for a considerable length of time. The OWC Elite Pro (minis) hard drives are little, can be transport controlled, tastefully coordinate my Apple items, and out of around 20-30 drives I've acquired for myself, customers, and companions, I've never had a solitary one turn sour. I can't suggest them enough.

Prepared to work? Contact your friends (once more) and take to the virtual worlds!

Quite a bit of my work has originated from other video makers or rehash customers, where I altered a venture once for them, conceivably at their area, and had the option to keep on working with them even subsequent to moving the nation over. It was as simple as telling them that I had the capacities to telecommute and that I could transfer alters for them. All they have to do is Fedex me a drive and I'll wrap up (pretty much!)

Makers I've worked for have alluded me to other people, so I've included a few customers from verbal exchange alone. Other than the previously mentioned, assets like Mandy.com, the Creative Cow Job Search, ProductionHub, and even here and there Craigslist have yeilded ventures. Facebook has turned into another way I've looked for some kind of employment also, by adding myself to gatherings identified with video or photography, and joining discussions when I saw a chance to network and offer my administrations.

Have a record sharing help prepared to utilize

Working remotely, I'll regularly get sent a hard drive with film. In the next week that I'm altering, unavoidably there will be some still photographs, illustrations, or different records I have to get from the maker. Great makers will more often than not have a record move administration set up, yet you may need to offer an answer too in the event that they don't. Google Drive or Box.com have functioned admirably for me previously. They are free and take care of business. In the event that you have your own FTP server for your site you can utilize that, and there are additionally administrations like Nimia.com that offer document moves and talk abilities, notwithstanding different highlights.

Work quick and quick

Makers have a lot of alternatives for video editors, and for them to work with somebody remotely you need to make it as simple as feasible for them, and give a speedy turnaround. This can mean working during that time to get an unpleasant slice to them the following morning. I'm 2 hours behind the east coast, so I'm either up late the principal night or up promptly the following morning to blast out a harsh cut before the accompanying work day is accomplished for my customers. I'd bet this is one reason I get rehash business.

Track your time.

On the off chance that charging continuously and not the task, I utilize a clock on my telephone as a kind of advanced punch clock. There are a few applications for both your work area and cell phone that can do this, so there's no explanation you can't follow your time. You will charge precisely, yet additionally get an extraordinary thought of to what extent it takes you to do alters, which will assist you with quoting employments better later on.

Use fares or renders to take breaks.

I do this constantly. I'll work until I hit a characteristic delay, either from rendering, sending out, or moving documents. While these run, I'll eat, take the canine out, or on account of sending out a long alter, I'll set it up to run medium-term. Thusly I'm not sitting around during business hours, when I could be accomplishing more work.

Mark, sort out, and make it sham verification.

In case you're a decent proofreader, odds are you do this as of now. On the hard drive your customer sends you, make an organizer named with your name and the task name. Inside it, subfolders isolating music, illustrations, venture records, and everything else, will help keep things perfect and sorted out for the person who opens this up on the customer end. I've been on phone calls with customers in the past in light of the fact that I didn't mark organizers appropriately and it made me look terrible when they couldn't locate a specific record. Exercise learned!

Use Vimeo for unpleasant cuts and even finished editions.

With a Vimeo Plus record, I'm ready to transfer recordings and secret phrase ensure them. I'll do this for harsh cuts on the activities I'm altering. Vimeo is a truly available spot to watch recordings from, and my customers can even download the document in the event that they have to.

Refreshing the video on vimeo with another alter form takes only a tick.

★ Make Money from Creating Animations Videos

The interest to make money with videos online has never been higher. Bloggers, new digital market platform, known media organizations and brands are shouting out for quality short movies. The animated films that can be streamed, keeping in mind the end goal are to manufacture glory. To gain refinement and direct people to their online networking or social media.

Can we make money with videos online?

While wanting to make a short film, there must be somebody who knows you came and make this Inquiry about: How to make money online with animated video? You at that point say a confused response to. Now we ask you: For what valid reason? Without expecting a budgetary advantage, why you want to know? What's more, why you didn't use the accessible business possibilities for gaining cash from your animated videos.

We realize that there are too many blogs that are purposed to show you about the approaches to profit from YouTube, no Budget filmmaking tips as such. While we chose to compose something about this point, one thing that we write about is– Never compose something that is not understandable.

In view of your film talk dialect region, start a joint effort with well running YouTube or Vemo channel that has a high volume of endorsers and begins a business association with all of them. Think about the partnership along ahead in long term.

Offering privileges for your animation video, influencing it as a component. if the fortunes support financer (Film Producer) will probably enables you to coordinate that film. Otherwise, you will get patent rights for utilizing the topic of the short film.

Are you decided to Create Animation Videos for YouTube Platform? Well, that is a great option for filmmakers and video creators to generate income from their videos. At present, the YouTube is having 1 billion users' presence and 300 hours of videos, upload to YouTube on Every Hour.

Numerous individuals pick filmmaking as their career and setting their minds to making cash is a basic thing. Making cash through filmmaking or animated videos isn't a straight street. You have to ensure quality work to win cash and be perceived. Developing short film industry now offers a bigger number of choices than it did a couple of years back. One can settle on the following approaches on how to make money online with animated video:

♣ Make your own YouTube channel and viral your video. Yet, this by itself isn't sufficient. You require no less than 80 people into your channel before you begin earning. Sites like YouTube search in terms for the number of subscribers.

♣ You can utilize online stages like Short fondly – A stage for creative movie producers or animated filmmakers to advance your work and pick up the crowd. To gain all the attention from your target audience.

♣ Participate in film celebrations. This will give you acknowledgement in the film business. As animation filmmaking is also growing day by day you can draw the attention towards your animated video.

♣ Post your animated videos at settled (well established) channels which will enable you to get viewers and supporters in extensive numbers. All that subscription in large number through a known site.

Most likely the simplest and least expensive answer for the less technically knowledgeable individuals, or for the individuals who do not have a large audience. For $199/year in addition to 10% of your profit, you'll have the capacity to sell your animated videos directly on Vimeo. Much the same as offering on Amazon, the huge preferred standpoint. The large number of viewers, willing to pay to watch quality movies. In the event that you don't have your own audience, adding yourself to an extensive accessible site (Searchable source) of movies may be a decent method to discover your clients or your target audience.

On the off chance that you have your own site, and have some sort of following. You can offer your animated videos specifically to them. There are numerous tools for offering advanced items, there are only a couple of them:

♣ Gum road

♣ Woo commerce

♣ Wistia

♣ Amazon S3

Nothing is impossible in this era, you can actually make money with videos online. Follow your passion for the animation and you can make money with videos online easily.

YouTube views:

This method is the simplest one, but probably the least effective. You make a short, upload it to YouTube, monetize your channel by enabling ads and watch the money flows.

Here's why it's not the most effective method, though: Let's say you make 2 animated shorts per year, which is INCREDIBLY hard to do. Then, let's say each short gets 5 Million views by some stroke of luck from the virality God. Your total revenue for that year will then be around $10,000. And again, that's with the unlikely scenario of managing to produce 2 very popular animated shorts in one year.

YouTube not a great platform for animators because it relies on watch time and frequency of uploads. These two factors create a lot of difficulty for animators, since it takes such a long time to create a short animation, and it's usually pretty short. That's one of the reasons gaming channels do so well, they upload almost every day and their videos can go on for a long long time.

However, there is a way an animation channel can do great on YouTube, and that's by creating content around your shorts. This is what I've done since the beginning.

Uploading making-of videos, tutorials and production-vlogs. If you only upload your shorts you will have a hard time getting traction, but if you create some momentum around it with other content, you will have an easier time growing on YouTube.

The more popular YouTube animators often resort to a limited animation style, more similar to an animatic, and almost always in 2D. That way they can produce much more videos. Here is the list of some of our favorite YouTube animation channels.

Selling your short

Selling your animated short directly to your audience can be much more profitable. Say you sell it for $5, you will only need 2000 views to get to that $10,000 figure we talked about earlier. But that also means you'll have to get 2000 people to buy your film, which isn't an easy task, especially if you haven't spent time building an audience.

When we launch our next short Tasteful it will be much easier for us to sell it (since we've been talking about it for such a long time and have been building a following for the past 3 years) compared to someone who simply releases their short out of thin air.

Here are some of the ways you can sell your short directly to your audience:

Vimeo on Demand

Probably the easiest and cheapest solution for the less tech-savvy people, or for those who does not have a large audience. For $199/year plus 10% of your earnings, you'll be able to sell your animated short directly on Vimeo. Just like selling on Amazon, the big advantage here is the exposure to a large pool of primed viewers, willing to pay to watch quality films. If you don't have your own audience, adding yourself to a large searchable source of films might be a good way to find your customers.

Amazon / iTunes

I don't have experience with selling on these platforms, but I know that many people use them. iTunes could get costly (sometimes paying thousands to aggregators for posting your film) and Amazon can be used for free. You'll have to do a bit more research on that if that's the path you think about taking.

Sell on you own site

This is something I have more experience with. If you have your own site, and have built some kind of following, you can sell your shorts directly to them. There are many tools for selling digital products, here are just a few I'm familiar with, either from personal use or from recommendations:

] Easy Digital Downloads (A shopping cart plugin for WordPress)

] Gumroad (A super easy-to-use tool for selling digital products)

] Woocommerce (The most popular shopping cart plugin)

] Wistia (A high-quality video hosting company, for hosting your animated short)

| Amazon S3 (Amazon's cloud storage tool, for
letting your customers download your film
to their computers)

Merchandize

An indirect way to make money from your film, having
merchandize could work for you, especially if your film is
on the cuter side, making plush dolls or pillow cases a
viable thing to sell. Sites like Society6 let you upload
designs and then sell a large verity of products with
those designs. Anything from mugs to posters to hoodies.

For example: When we release Tasteful we will be selling
an art-of book with concept art, character designs etc. This
would be a great accompanying product for the film,
providing great value to the viewer as well as helping us
maintain a sustainable business

2 EARN MONEY FROM SIMPLE JOB

★ **Earn Money From Simple Jobs**

•Virtual Assistant

With so many businesses operating mostly, or even completely, online, it's no wonder that many hire virtual assistants to help keep them organized and complete administrative tasks. According to the International Virtual Assistants Association, these workers are "independent contractors who (from a remote location, usually their home or office) support multiple clients in a variety of industries by providing administrative, creative, and technical services."

Although virtual assistant jobs vary drastically, tasks can include composing and responding to emails, creating and distributing business-related documents, responding to media and business inquiries, writing and creating content, and more. Check out virtual assistant jobs at sites such as Upwork.com and Zirtual.com.

While pay varies, virtual assistants can typically charge between $15 and $75 an hour. However, what you'll earn depends on who you work for and the level of skill required for your daily tasks.

Anybody can turn into a menial helper and get paid to do what they cherish. I've demonstrated it!

One of the main dollars I at any point earned as an online entrepreneur was by working for another business person as her Marketing Assistant.

I advanced her digital books through looking into and making posts for visitor blogging efforts, making points of arrival for online courses, composing follow up email groupings for pamphlets, and dealing with her web based life stages.

If I somehow managed to begin my online business once more I'd at present do it a similar way!

Working for a progressively experienced business person enabled me to become familiar with the ropes, see in the background of her business, and approach her cerebrum. She tutored me as well as it resembled I got paid to learn!

That is the best part about making cash as somebody's remote helper, overseeing editorial manager, or venture supervisor. You gain admittance to the internal functions of their business all while getting paid.

In case you're hoping to turn into a remote helper, and make cash helping different entrepreneurs, presently's ideal time to start.

Remember to snatch this free manual for 150+ administrations you can offer as a remote helper! Turning into a menial helper with no experience
At the point when I initially propelled this blog in 2011 I truly had no clue what I was doing. I mishandled around, composed a couple of blog entries, and posted a couple of tweets on Twitter. It wasn't until I ardently begun perusing different online journals about business and enterprise that my vocation improved.

In the wake of pursuing a few bulletin records and "stalking" a couple of business people via web-based networking media, I handled the gig a couple of days after the fact! We worked out an installment bargain where I got paid $16 an hour for around 32 hours of work every month. The rate and work expanded after some time and I in the end moved to a month to month retainer plan that worked out to generally $25 60 minutes. I worked with this customer for 2.5 years and she gave me a sparkling tribute. In case you're figuring it out, $16 an hour X 32 hours every month = $512 in my first month!

That's right, inside my first month of being a remote helper I had the option to acquire over $500! Furthermore, this return in 2012 so envision the amount more cash you could win now.

Here are the means you can profit as an amateur menial helper in only 30 days.

1. Land your first customer
Finding your first customer is startling — you're putting yourself out there and feel like you have no cracking thought what you're doing.

Uncertainty begins to sneak in and you're asking why on the planet anybody would pay you for your ability and aptitudes.

This is the reason it's savvy to begin as a VA by utilizing a sidelong ability.

I don't get this' meaning? The fastest method to begin getting paid is to advertise an ability you definitely know. This can be founded on past involvement, a vocation confirmation, or past information.

Transform something you definitely realize how to do into the establishment for your VA business. In the event that you went to class for bookkeeping, start an accounting or advanced association business.

Influence your past experience to grandstand abilities that are as of now in your resume.

2. Offer VA administrations customers need

When you have a potential activity you need to apply for, you need an outline of administrations or bundles of your present contributions. There are truly unlimited assignments and administrations you can offer to different business visionaries: Email the board Web based life booking
Showcasing and online classes Blog the board Digital book advancement and visitor blogging, Independent composition Altering and copywriting Looking into and actuality checking The rundown goes on… Restricted down your concentration by just offering 1-3 bundles dependent on past experience and stir your way up from that point. Rundown the essential errands for each, start/end dates, what each bundle + rate incorporates, any installment subtleties, a customer tribute, and a connect to your portfolio.

3. Make a site or portfolio

When you have your lord rundown of VA administrations you can utilize this to help make the bundles/contributions on a site or portfolio page.
On the off chance that you don't have a Services page or the like it's an ideal opportunity to set one up. This can be known as a "work with me" page, "enlist me" page, or whatever else.
You need to give potential customers a spot to see your contributions and check whether you're a solid match, just as making it idiotically simple for them to get in touch with you. The less taps the better!

Two instances of changing over Service pages:
Look at Kristin's Hire Me page. She took a shot at unmistakably characterizing her bundles, streamlining her page, and setting her rates. Also, as a result of this she as of late had her best pay month yet!

My Hire Me page is upgraded for the hunt term "remote helper" so when anybody types that expression into Google, my page is one of the primary outcomes.
An agenda for your Service page to turn into a menial helper:
What your identity is and what you offer (in addition to what you don't!)
Past experience, models, portfolio Present and past customers Contributions, administrations, bundles Points, industry, and so on Current rates (or beginning rates)
Tributes from current customers A contact structure

4. Charge continuously versus a level rate

In the first place phases of offering VA benefits it's ideal to charge customers constantly. It's hard to completely see how rapidly you work and to what extent certain ventures will take you.
Try not to place yourself in the situation of working for a considerable length of time and days and not getting appropriately made up for it.
When you realize to what extent the sorts of administrations you offer take you, and the aggregate sum of work they involve, you should change to a month to month expense or level rate as opposed to charging continuously.
For email the executives work you may definitely realize that it will take you 1-2 hours out of each day, 5 days per week, so you could offer this administration for a level $400 every week (which works out to be $40 60 minutes).

Snap here to turn into a menial helper today!

Some VA work is simpler to pinpoint how a lot of work is included while others are increasingly conceptual and will take some experimentation.

The going rate for VA work begins at $20 every hour and can be as much as $50 every hour. You can acknowledge a much lower rate however more often than not this is possibly shrewd in case you're very unpracticed. After that it's imperative to build your costs and request raises consistently.

The more specific your VA contributions are, the more every hour you can charge. It likewise relies upon your customer and their industry of work.

A non-benefit customer won't have the option to manage the cost of about as much as a money related organization can. Try not to be hesitant to begin charging constantly and afterward change to a level rate.

This will enable you to have more opportunity with how you invest your energy, and cut back on your administrator hours when making solicitations toward the month's end.

5. Learn constantly

A significant piece of turning into a remote helper is that you're continually learning and improving your specialty. Online entrepreneurs and business visionaries frequently need assistance with tech-related issues and testing out new social stages or business devices.

What's more, YOU can be the one to assist them with this! Nonetheless, so as to do this adequately it's imperative to learn constantly. You ought to normally be putting resources into yourself, sharpening your aptitudes, and expanding your insight. This should be possible through tuning in to digital broadcasts, perusing business books, and putting resources into classes and courses.

Step by step instructions to turn into a remote helper

In case you're prepared to begin acquiring your first $500 this month, here are the means to take; Locate your optimal customer and tail them via web-based networking media Influence past involvement to arrive your first customer

Concoct an ace rundown of administrations to offer as a remote helper

Set up together an unmistakable Services page or portfolio Upgrade your Services page for the best outcomes Charge continuously then move to a level rate Keep expanding your rates and costs Furthermore, you can begin at the present time! Download the free manual for 150+ Virtual Assistant Services to Offer Clients. Making a move today will enable you to kick off your VA profession so you can begin accomplishing your fantasies about bringing home the bacon from home.

•Medical Transcriptionist

Although many medical transcriptionists work for hospitals or physician's offices, most are able to work at home, and at a time or place of their choosing. Since their tasks involve transcribing recorded medical dictation, a computer, desk, and earpiece are generally the only requirements after completing a postsecondary medical transcriptionist program.

According to the Bureau of Labor Statistics (BLS), medical transcriptionists earned a national median wage of $35,720 in May of 2016, or $17.17 an hour. Although many medical transcriptionists are self-employed, many find jobs through their local hospital, physician, or community college or vocational school.

•Translator

According to the Bureau of Labor Statistics, most translators do their work at home, and often under tight deadlines. Although some need a bachelor's degree, the most important requirement for translators is, of course, fluency in at least two languages.

As the BLS notes, around 22% of translators were self-employed in 2016. The majority were spread among these industries: professional, scientific, and technical services (30%); state, local, and private educational services (23%); hospitals (8%); and government (6%).

The national median wage for this career was $46,120 in 2016, although the top 10% of workers earned an average of $83,010. Look for job postings for translators on sites like Upwork.com.
Web Developer

•Travel Agent

Although the demand is expected to decrease over the next decade, the opportunities are still there for travel agents who can harness the Internet to earn clients and help them plan their adventures. According to the BLS, job prospects may be best for travel agents who offer expertise in certain regions of the world, have experience planning tours or adventures, or who focus on group travel. Around 15% of travel agents were self-employed in 2016, but the vast majority of the rest of them worked in the travel arrangement and reservation services industry. Travel agents earned a national median wage of $36,460 in 2016.

★ Freelance Writer

More than ever, writers are needed to formulate news articles, create content, and come up with the creative ideas that fill the pages of nearly every site on the Internet. And although many bigger sites have in-house writers, a growing number of sites outsource their content and hire freelance writers and content creators. Writing experience is very helpful, but what you really need to get started are drive, ambition, and the ability to find a unique angle on events that happen every day.

Sites like Upwork.com list online freelancing positions, as does Freelancer.com and Media Bistro. To get hired, you'll likely need to have a portfolio of solid work, or at least some writing samples you can include with your resume. While writing fees vary depending on the job and the freelancer, many writers earn at least $150 per article and some earn up to $1,500 per finished piece. The BLS notes that writers earned a median wage of $61,240 nationally in 2016, although the top ten percent of workers earned around $118,640.

What You'll Need so as to Make Money Freelancing Online

Abilities People Want to Buy

A consultant is a person who performs administrations for a charge, regardless of whether that is hourly, per word, or per venture. At the end of the day, specialists exchange time for cash.

In this manner, you have to have abilities individuals are eager to pay for. You can get innovative here! Such huge numbers of individuals figure they don't have the experience to turn into a specialist, however I challenge you to survey your history.

Have you at any point had work? Assuming this is the case, that implies you DO have aptitudes individuals will pay you for! The most straightforward change from representative to specialist is to begin with the things you've just been paid to do.

For instance, before I turned into a consultant, I was chipping away at the advertising group of a startup. So when I chose to go independent, what did I do? I began selling advertising administrations (web-based social networking the board, copywriting, PR crusades, and so on.) to new companies! It was a basic progress since I could utilize the work I did as a worker as my portfolio as a consultant.

In the event that regardless you think you do not have the right stuff to turn into a specialist, there is a sort of outsourcing work you ought to thoroughly consider: being a remote helper.

I think about the menial helper as the passage level occupation in the independent world. Much like a secretary can proceed to turn into the workplace chief, a menial helper can proceed to turn into an online business administrator, an advertising expert, a website specialist, and extremely some other "more elevated level" independent position!

What's a remote helper? A remote helper helps an individual or business with practically any assistance possible. There are remote helpers for:

•travel booking

•appointment planning

•email the board

•graphic plan

•social media the board

•proofreading

For instance, suppose you need to be an expert independent supervisor, however you've just done a couple altering occupations and don't feel you're able to be a full-time independent editorial manager. You can begin as a menial helper who offers editing administrations. The thing that matters is that you'll get paid not exactly on the off chance that you were an independent manager, however in the end, you can elevate yourself to proofreader and charge a higher rate since you'll have assembled your portfolio as a menial helper.

Activity STEP: If you've thought hard everything you could, yet come up short on the abilities to turn into a specialist: adapt new aptitudes by means of online courses!

Some Ideas from top courses:

•Pinterest Traffic Avalanche – This will support you in the event that you'd like to deal with business' Pinterest records to enable them to direct people to their locales and, at last, make more income. I've taken this course and prescribe it!

•Making Sense of Affiliate Marketing – This will support you in the event that you'd like to turn into a partner director helping bloggers and different organizations increment their subsidiary income. I've taken this course as well. Look at my audit of it.

•Earn More Writing – This will support you on the off chance that you'd like to turn into an independent essayist. The course was made by a functioning independent essayist who makes six figures from her composition work.

•30 Days or Less to Freelance Writing Success – Another independent composition course that will tell you the best way to transform your composition abilities into a business quick.

•30 Days or Less to Virtual Assistant Success – An incredible method to break into outsourcing is through turning into a remote helper. VAs are required by bloggers, specialists, independent companies and even enormous organizations. You can do anything from regulatory to plan to composing work.

A Reliable Internet Connection

In case you will work remotely as a specialist, you will require a solid Internet association. For my kindred Americans and others in the First World, this is normally not an issue. It turns into an issue, in any case, on the off chance that you choose to travel while working.

At whatever point I travel to progressively remote regions, I have a few alternatives helpful to get to Internet out and about:

•   T-Mobile

- Verizon JetPack

On the other hand, you can simply adhere to computerized wanderer well disposed spots. On the off chance that you need to go off-the-framework, ensure you complete your work early and take an appropriate get-away —free of any independent work.

A Personal Computer / Laptop

You could utilize a personal computer, yet in the event that you'll be in a hurry a ton, a workstation is a superior choice. I utilize this PC, and it's been ideal for my run of the mill assignments, which include:

- Typing in Google Docs
- Editing pictures in Photoshop
- Light video altering with Camtasia
- Sending messages
- Transcribing sound
- Uploading pictures to WordPress

A Domain / Website

As an online specialist, you need a site. This is your "online customer facing facade," and in addition to the fact that it serves as your portfolio, it additionally demonstrates you're genuine.

In spite of mainstream thinking, it doesn't cost a great deal of cash and you don't must have coding abilities to dispatch a site. Indeed, you can even form your independent site for FREE.

Instructions to Make Money Freelancing Online in 7 Steps

Stage 1: Decide what you will sell.

Sounds basic enough, isn't that so? As I discussed above, you'll have to assess what aptitudes you have and how you can transform those into administrations individuals will need to purchase.

Stage 2: Decide who you need to work with (your optimal customers).

Know your circle and work with the best candidates, hire experienced Person with the right expertise for your work.

Stage 3: Price and bundle your administrations.

Making sense of how to value your administrations as a consultant will be one of the most difficult and essential things you do while setting up your independent business. I obsessed about my rates for a considerable length of time when I began. I likewise seriously undervalued my administrations in the first place, to such an extent that I was working continually yet always broke.

(Individual costs + operational expense + reserve funds)/. 7 = Revenue Goal

The .7 speaks to 70%, as in, 30% goes to expenses, and you keep 70% to use for yourself. Presently, annual duties are entangled and fluctuate generally. Most specialists inform putting aside 25% with respect to your independent pay to settle regulatory expenses. On the off chance that you make more than the normal specialist, 30% might be better (it additionally relies upon where you live). Be that as it may, I've discovered that 30% is all that anyone could need. On the off chance that you spare TOO a lot, it's route superior to sparing close to nothing!

Since the title of this post is the means by which to make your $5,000/month as a consultant, we'll use $5,000 every month for instance target objective. In the event that you make $5,000 in REVENUE, that implies that after 30% of assessments is taken out, you get the opportunity to keep $3,500 in PROFIT.

Along these lines, for this model, ensure your own costs, operational expense, and whatever sum you put in a safe spot for reserve funds doesn't surpass $3,500. On the off chance that it does, at that point your objective income very to be higher than $5K.

Stage 4: Create your site.

You NEED a portfolio site to prevail upon customers as a consultant. Be that as it may, it doesn't need to cost a lot of cash. You can even make a portfolio site for nothing. In case you're an independent essayist, you can utilize Contently to make a free portfolio site that exhibits your connections.

Stage 5: Find perfect potential customers (prospecting)

Presently, you have to go out and make a rundown of potential customers alongside their contact data (email address and first name is fine).

In case you're trapped, here are 11 spots online to discover independent gigs:

- AngelList
- Working Nomads

- Flexjobs
- RemoteOK.io
- Facebook gatherings
- Craigslist
- Cold messaging your preferred brands
- Friends and family
- Your expert system or different specialists
- Your boss or past businesses

Stage 6: Pitch them (outbound promoting)

While I'm a fanatic of inbound advertising, when you're simply beginning, you don't have the opportunity to squander. You should pitch potential customers forcefully.

State 7: Conduct disclosure calls

When you've pitched some potential customers, you ought to hear over from a few. Now, it's a great opportunity to book a revelation call or beginning interview. This is fundamentally where you jump on the telephone (or video talk) with a prospect and attempt to choose in case you're a solid match for one another.

Presently, don't get frightened, however this is a business call. In addition to the fact that you want to choose in case you're a solid match, yet you additionally need to let the big dog eat on the off chance that you conclude that you are.

Numerous new specialists have revelation call tension. Everything I can say is that I did as well, and it improves time and practice. The more revelation calls you do, the more calm you will feel.

Stage 8: Negotiate

No entrepreneur is insusceptible to exchange. It's the name of the game, and as a consultant, you should generally expect it.

Here are a couple of potential situations and how you can respond:

•If the customer needs to consult on cost: Except for unique cases, I'm a firm devotee that you ought to NEVER consult on cost, just on SCOPE. That implies if your charge for a 5-page site is $3,000, yet the customer demands they can just bear the cost of $2K, at that point possibly you chop it down to a 3-page site.

•If the customer needs to consult on extension: Be available to this current; it's thoroughly fine! Simply make sure to alter your charges as needs be.

•If the customer needs to consult on course of events: You reserve each privilege to charge a surge expense if a customer needs something done rapidly.

•If the customer isn't sure they need to work with you: Tread cautiously. Vulnerability some of the time can be a warning for an issue customer—one who continually changes scope on you and makes you overhaul and reconsider in light of the fact that they're not in any case sure what they need. Nonetheless, once in a while, they're amazing customers—they simply need all the more persuading that YOU are the correct specialist for them. In those cases, I offer a shorter paid time for testing. Thump it out of the recreation center during the paid preliminary, and they'll be anxious to keep on working with you. You can likewise offer a free preliminary or an unconditional promise.

•If the customer needs to attach additional administrations outside of what you ordinarily offer: Tread cautiously. If its all the same to those additional administrations are something you offering, I state let it all out, yet make certain to attach additional charges for it! On the off chance that those additional administrations are something you would prefer not to offer, at that point hold fast.

•Social Media Manager

Almost every big business has gotten on the social media bandwagon as a means to reach their customers directly, and without paying heavily for television, print, or radio ads. But not every big business has someone to manage their social media accounts, which is why more individuals have begun marketing themselves as social media managers and helping businesses grow their online following and expand their reach.
Although very little data are available for this work-at-home job since it is relatively new, thousands of listings for social media managers can be found on sites like CareerBuilder.com, SimplyHired.com, and Upwork.com. If you have a demonstrated command of social media and a sizable following, you might even be able to get started by reaching out to companies directly and asking if they need help.
Social media managers typically earn the same as a virtual assistant, with hourly rates of $15 – $75 fairly common. Some social media managers also work for a retainer or monthly fee, however.

★Data Entry Jobs
wide range of businesses need workers to enter various data into their systems, whether that data are used to track inventory or shipments, create business plans, or measure performance or output. And since a computer and typing skills are the most important requirements for this job,

many data entry workers are able to work at home, and on a schedule that fits their lives.

According to the BLS, data entry workers earned a national median wage of $30,100 in 2016, although the top 10% earned more like $45,360. Since many data entry jobs are at-home jobs, you can always find dozens of data entry job postings on sites like Upwork.com, Freelancer.com, and SimplyHired.com, as well as dozens of others.

1. Captcha Entry Job

Captcha entry is becoming one of the hottest online data entry job. Although income is less than other job but its very simple & available for everyone.

You will be given a software where you have to login with your username & password & then type the Captcha images. You can earn up to $500 per month from this job.

2. Copy & Paste

Here you have to copy text material from a word or excel file and paste into another word or excel file. It is very easy however, you need to be very careful. Good knowledge of English is very important because you have to read and understand things.

3. Micro Jobs

There are number of sites where you can join as a micro worker & work on different types of data task. One of the most recommended online data entry job for extra income.

There are dozens of sites that provide micro jobs where you can join & earn minimum $200+ a month working on simple tasks.

4. Survey Forms

Filling up survey forms is also a type of data entry work. Here you have to fill online forms provided by different survey sites.

Through this form, you give your feedback for a particular product which helps companies to design the best products for consumers.

5. Basic Typing Job

The first and basic data entry job is typing. Here you have to type anything into an excel spreadsheet or a word document.

You don't require any special skill other than typing speed of 30+ words per minute. If your speed is less than this & you want to do this then you have to improve the speed to reach 30+ WPM level.

6. Form Filling

Form filling data entry jobs are not very common but you can find them on Internet. Here you have to fill simple forms with given information. Sometimes information is not given and you have to find on your own.

7. Image to Text

Next is converting image to text. Here you have an image file containing text material and you need to write it down on a word document. To put it simple, you have to see from image file and write it down on a word document.

8. Medical Transcription

Medical Transcription is the most popular work from home job. Here you have to be on a phone and write things down what you listen. So it is bit different than regular data entry job. You need great listening skills and write it down as you listen.

9. Formatting

You have to format a word document. Formatting is not that easy as it is seen. You have to have full knowledge of work documents, things like indentation, aligning etc.So learn MS word.

10. Content Writing

Content writing is bit different than regular data entry job. Here you have to write articles and give it back to publishers. Here you need more of a writing skill than typing skills.

11. Catalog Data Entry Operator

Catalog data entry operator is about creating an inventory list in an excel spreadsheet. An inventory has many products and you have to write it down their serial number, product name, numbers in stock, price etc into an excel spreadsheet.

This is like a normal data entry job.

12. Proofreading and Copywriting

Like content writing proofreading and copywriting is also a data entry work. However, they are bit different than regular data entry jobs.

Here you have to good at English and typing speed is not required. You must be able to read articles and find out mistakes.

13. Medical Coding

Medical coding is data entry work where you have to write codes of various products. These products are medicine of different kinds.

You have to be careful while entering those medical codes. You need some experience to take this job.

14. Payroll Data Entry Operator

Payroll data entry operator is for creating a payroll list for various companies. You have to create a list of employee name, address, salary etc in Excel spreadsheet.

The job is very similar to the catalog data entry operator where you fill information about products in the inventory.

15. Email Processing

Email processing jobs are about processing emails. You have to read emails and find out what their content is about. You might be asked to process thousands of email in a day. The job could be very exciting.

Extra:- Customized Data Entry Jobs

This is not actually a specific kind of data entry jobs. Here you could be asked to do anything what a company has to say.

The job is not specified and customized according to the needs of the company. You job could be anything.

So these were some of the data entry jobs available on the Internet and offline. You need to find out more about these online jobs and prepare yourself to become a data entry operator.

★ Call-Center Representative
Many businesses need workers who can answer the phone at all hours, assist customers, and process orders or deal with returns. But since more businesses are operating

online, a growing number of these jobs are going to customer service workers who work at home.

Being an at-home call-center rep requires a computer and may require specific software or equipment. A great phone voice helps as well, as does any experience in customer service, data entry, retail sales, or management. Dozens of sites list job openings for call-center representatives, including Upwork.com, Freelancer.com, and SimplyHired.com. However, you may also find listings offered by local businesses in your local newspaper. While it's hard to find exact pay for call center representatives who work at home, Glassdoor.com says this workers typically earn a base pay of around $30,000 per year.

How does a job where you can work from home and get paid to talk on the phone sounds to you?

If you're used to telephone work, then an at home customer service agent job could be an excellent way to make money.

The company is called VOIQ, and the job is making calls on behalf of major companies to people who have already expressed an interest in hearing from them – no cold calls.

You can set your own hours with no minimum requirement, and like any other legitimate work at home job, it doesn't cost you anything to get started.

What You Need to Know?

As a VOIQ agent, you take on the role of a professional call agent, but don't have the hassle of going to work in a call center. In fact, you can do your job from anywhere as long as you have certain things:

) you must have a smartphone, and it can be iPhone or Android

) you need a good Internet connection

) you must be over 21

) you should be experienced at working in a call center

You will also need to have a relatively quiet space in which to work uninterrupted during the hours you choose. It's important that you are professional in taking on this task, as you will represent the employing company to the public.

Of course, there may be time restrictions on when you can call the customers. Typically you would need to do your work between 8 AM and 6 PM, though it may depend on what time zones you and the customers are in.

For its part, VOIQ is the company employing you, which provides the necessary app and software for you to work, and gets the jobs from the various employing companies.

VOIQ typically asks its applicants for 2 to 5 years prior experience in a call center.

How You Can Apply

You apply online at voiq.com, filling out your personal details and answering some yes or no questions, such as "Do you have a quiet place to work from?" and "Do you have an Android device, iPhone or iPad?".

You then have to record some 60-second videos using the camera in your computer and answering relevant questions related to your previous and intended work.

It seems like there is no way to skip this step, so if you don't have a camera on your computer, you will need to borrow a friend's.

You're also required to submit your resume in order for them to review your application. In the TOS, they make it clear that they don't even review you until they have a resume in hand.

After that, it can take up to three days to hear back.

Whether they decide to employ you will obviously depend on your performance and speaking voice, as well as having the right answers to the mainly obvious questions.

What You Have To Do

You work with the mobile app which you can download from the iTunes App Store or the Google Play Store.

VOIQ will email you every time a new campaign starts, and you can go from there.

The app will give you a short tutorial guide for the particular campaign, telling you what to say, ask, or do. You need to become sufficiently familiar with this that it will sound natural when you talk to the customer.

After each call, you have to mark the call outcome.

This can be

  ] Busy

  ] Number no longer in service

  ] No one answered the phone

  ] Message delivered to voicemail

  ] Contact can't be reached at this number

  ] Contact requested to not be called again

  ] Contact asked to be called later

With some campaigns, you don't leave a voicemail, but mark the call as "asked to be called later" so that the contact is made at a later date.

How Much Do You Get Paid?

For your work, you will be paid $12 per hour, provided you work consistently.

This is equivalent to about $.30 per minute (for every phone call,) allowing time between calls.

You can get paid any time you've earned at least one dollar in your account.

VOIQ does not send out money on any regular schedule, you have to ask for it. The money arrives by PayPal a few days later.

Be aware that your recorded calls may be listened to by the Quality Assurance team before they approve and pay you. If you have worked in a call center, you will be familiar with the idea of supervisors listening in on your calls at random to make sure you're doing a good job – this is a similar idea for the remote application. VOIQ has to be sure that it maintains standards, in order to satisfy its clients.

Is It for You?

If you have some experience working in a call center, this may be the ideal opportunity. No longer do you have to fight through traffic to sit in one of many cubicles, but you can work this job from home or any other quiet place.

You have to be diligent and able to work without a set schedule, and have a pleasant professional approach to the task. Your work will be reviewed, and the best call agents will tend to have new work offered to them first, so it's worth making an effort.

In return, the rewards are decent and you get all the freedom that you want, doing a job that you are good at.

If you meet the qualifications, visit VOIQ and apply for their at home customer service agent position and start getting paid. Even if you do it part time, it still is a great way to earn some side income

★Blogger

Becoming a blogger is unlike any other work-at-home job in that you have to show up and build it yourself. Even worse, the vast majority of blogs make zero dollars for years as they grow and become established. In that sense, blogging isn't much of a job at all.

However, there is a lot of potential for writers who are able to build an audience, grow their site, and find a way to monetize it and start earning an income. Some of the ways bloggers make money include affiliate advertising, sponsored posts, Google Adsense, and product sales. Even better, owning a blog can be an inexpensive way to start your own business, with domains costing an average of $12 per year and Web hosting costing as little as $7.99 per month.

. Start a blog and make money

1. Building Your Readership

There are bunches of approaches to adapt your blog once you have a decent number of guests. In any case, when you are simply beginning you won't have numerous perusers, so it's imperative to benefit as much as possible from every one. That implies that you have to ensure first-time perusers of your blog will return. Just by having returning perusers will you ever fabricate a sizable group of spectators that you can benefit from.

So how might you keep in contact with your perusers?

The most effortless and most ideal route is to approach them for an email address where you can reach them with updates. By gathering your perusers' email addresses from the earliest starting point of your blog you will manufacture the greatest mailing list conceivable.

Ever wonder why pretty much every site you go to requests you to join with your email address?

In showcasing there is an adage that "the cash is in the mailing list". This is on the grounds that a mailing rundown enables you to contact individuals again and again.

Each time you send an email to your rundown you can offer them items/administrations or simply get them to your visit your blog again where you can profit from advertisements (talked about beneath). This is actually what enormous organizations like Groupon do with their mailing records. They convey offers on a day by day or week by week premise

You will require an email showcasing administration to begin. By a wide margin the least demanding and most dependable that I have found is Constant Contact, which offers a free preliminary of their administrations for new bloggers. I have assembled a total bit by bit instructional exercise on the most proficient method to utilize Constant Contact with your blog.

2. Adapting Your Blog

When you have manufactured a nice readership base you can direct your concentration toward profiting from your blog. There an assortment of approach to do this, however one of the most worthwhile ways additionally happens to be the least demanding publicizing.

Having an enormous number of guests to your blog implies that publicists will pay to have their advertisements appeared to your perusers. The most effortless approach to blog for cash is to get paid for indicating commercials on your blog by joining Google's AdSense program at http://www.google.com/adsense

When you arrangement your record on AdSense you will be given a code to add to your blog. This code will naturally show notices on your blog from organizations who are a piece of Google's publicizing system. You may see promotions from little organizations identified with your theme, or you may see advertisements from enormous organizations that are totally inconsequential to your point.

The decent thing about AdSense is that you have a large number of promoters offering to publicize on your blog, and you should simply add the basic code to your blog. When you do that the procedure is totally distant.

Each time one of your guests taps on an advertisement, you get paid. Google gathers the cash from the promoters and after that writes you a check (typically consistently).

This game plan is decent in light of the fact that it is hands-off, but since you are managing a legitimate organization that you realize will really pay you on schedule.

What amount would you be able to make?

The sum that you can make from AdSense relies upon three variables:

1. The quantity of guests to your blog

This one is really self-evident. More individuals visiting your blog implies more taps on promotions, which means more cash for you.

2. The perceivability of the advertisements

At the point when you put the AdSense code on your blog you have a decision of the style of notices (huge pictures, little pictures, content, and so forth.) and furthermore where they are put. The more unmistakably the promotions are shown the almost certain they are to be clicked.

Notwithstanding, you need to adjust setting the promotions noticeably with the possibility of conceivably irritating your peruses. We have all visited sites where it's hard to see the substance because of the number and size of the advertisements. This is a sensitive equalization to accomplish and it's something you should try different things with to benefit from your blog.

3. The theme you are blogging about

The last factor that influences your AdSense pay is the point you are blogging about. This is on the grounds that publicists will pay more to be on sure web journals than they will for other people.

For instance, if your site is about golf, your perusers are probably going to have a sound pay. Along these lines, there are a decent number of publicists that need to get their promotions before your perusers, and they are probably going to pay a decent sum for every snap to do this.

Balance this with a blog about Justin Bieber. The perusers of this blog are probably going to be young ladies, who more often than not have relatively little buying force. In view of this promoters will probably save money on each snap.

These three elements will decide the measure of cash you make. Evaluating precisely what you will make is entirely troublesome, yet a high traffic blog on the correct subject can possibly get a few thousand dollars consistently. Obviously, numerous individuals procure not as much as this, and some acquire significantly more. Truth be told, it has been assessed that some top AdSense distributers gain about $2 million every year just from AdSense.

Remember that creation cash from your blog requires some serious energy. All things considered, there is an explanation that figuring out how to profit from a blog is the last advance in my guide. You have to ensure you have pursued all the past advances splendidly so as to give yourself the most obvious opportunity with regards to acquiring a considerable salary from blogging. This won't occur without any forethought, yet most bloggers find that the work itself is compensating enough to proceed on the adventure.

When you have your blog ready for action, make a point to look at my bit by bit instructional exercise on the most proficient method to introduce AdSense on your blog.

As a new blogger, it can be hard to know where to start. You hear people are making money from their blogs, but you don't quite understand how.
In this beginner's guide on how to make money with a blog for beginners, we're going to show you how to make your first $100 from your blog.

I know. $100 doesn't sound like a lot of money. But it's just the beginning. Once you get the basics down and earn your first income, you can scale it and earn as much money as you'd like.

Here is Even more with Make Money as a Blogger

First of all, it's significant for me to advise you that blog salary doesn't occur incidentally. You should set up a blog, fabricate a group of people who trusts you and drive traffic routinely before you can begin making a salary. The intriguing blogger's way of life that you see via web-based networking media accompanies a ton of diligent work so prepare sure you're to placed the work in. As a blogger learner, you most likely don't have huge amounts of traffic yet and don't have a colossal email list either. So the thought here is to begin little ($100) and develop from that point as your blog develops in size.

By defining yourself a reasonable objective of $100, you will feel roused – as a bigger objective may appear to be excessively out of sight reach. Also, when you do accomplish your objective, you will improve comprehension of what works for your blog (and what doesn't) and utilize the learnings to get significantly more cash-flow.

The most effective method to Start a Blog in Under 10 Minutes

•Blog Niches That Make Money: 5 Profitable Blog Niche Ideas (Examples Included)

•What Should I Blog About? 80+ Ideas You Can Create a Blog About

•How To Come Up With a Blog Name. 8 Creative Ideas To Pick The Perfect Name

This post may contain member joins. In the event that you click on them and buy something we get a little level of the deal. More information here

Blogging For Money – For Beginners So in any case, how DO you make cash blogging as a tenderfoot? Indeed, there are really various ways you could approach this. Give me a chance to separate them for you.

1. Offshoot Income

One of the least demanding and most basic approaches to make cash blogging, for fledglings, is member advertising. You don't have to have your very own items or administrations. You essentially advance other individuals' items on your blog, and when somebody makes a buy, you make a commission off it.

Where to Find Affiliate Programs

So where do you discover these associate projects? To be straightforward there are many choices and it might overpower when you're beginning.

Numerous new bloggers start by profiting with Amazon. So you sign up to turn into an Amazon Affiliate and use connects inside your blog. At the point when somebody makes a buy on Amazon, you will make a little commission of it.

Furthermore, you can join to utilize enormous member advertising systems. These systems have a great many offshoot programs for an assortment of brands. You can pick the brands and items you need to advance and do it from one brought together stage.

Two partner promoting systems we use ourselves:

1.   ShareASale
2.   Commission Junction

1. Make a rundown of items and administrations you adore and use. Research potential affiilate advertising open doors for these.

2. Sign up to Amazon and additionally partner advertising systems.

3. Conceptualize and make content that will enable you to advance your picked items and administrations.

For instance, in case you're advancing a product you like you use, you could make an instructional exercise on the most proficient method to utilize the product (for amateurs). Inside this article, you would utilize your member interface for the product so in the event that somebody navigates and makes a buy, you make the commission.

You could likewise do item audits as a bit of substance. This is a technique many style and magnificence blogger use. They will compose a survey of items they like to utilize and after that incorporate an associate connection so their perusers can make a buy.

There are numerous inventive and successful approaches to make content that brings subsidiary showcasing results. Do your examination and perceive how different bloggers in your specialty are advancing their subsidiary organizations.

Try not to be hesitant to acquire thoughts and imitate effective bloggers. You don't have to rehash an already solved problem.

4. Advance your substance. For you to profit from offshoot openings, your blog should be perused. Advance your substance via web-based networking media, by means of your email list and anyplace else that is important. The more traffic you manufacture, the more the open doors for you to make partner salary.

2. Digital books

In the event that you need to sell your own items, a digital book is an incredible method to make cash blogging. It's additionally an incredible method to see whether your crowd is prepared to purchase from you.

Try not to get overpowered! A digital book is certainly not a novel. You don't need to compose several pages. Truth be told, most great digital books are succinct yet stuffed with data.

Think about a digital book as a more drawn out structure blog entry. You can make a digital book about practically any subject however clearly it would bode well to make it about a theme that is important to your perusers.

You should simply ensure it's a subject you know well and can expound on. What's more, obviously, it's a theme that is fascinating enough for your perusers to purchase from you.

Most apprentice bloggers will sell their first digital books at an entirely sensible cost. In this way, it's a smart thought to costs yours at $7 to $40 mark. That way, it is anything but a gigantic speculation for anybody to buy and you can sell it effectively.

Furthermore, for you... when you make a couple digital book deals, it's a colossal certainty sponsor. You know you're destined for success. You have individuals who need to purchase from you – you are currently prepared to take it to the following level.

When you've sold some digital books, you can take it further by making other advanced items, for example, online courses, video instructional exercises and furthermore online courses (which we talk about straightaway)

1. Conceptualize content thoughts: Analyze what substance reverberates with your group of spectators. What do they like finding out about? What subjects do you have skill in? What point connects with your group of spectators the most?

Ask yourself these inquiries to pick a digital book point that will

2. Compose the digital book: Keep things basic. You needn't bother with any extravagant programming. Start composing and organizing your digital book in Google Docs. You can structure an alluring spread utilizing Canva and you're all set.

3. Make sense of where to sell: To sell your digital book, you can utilize a wide range of stages:

1. All alone blog: Promote it wherever on your blog. Set up pennants in the sidebar, notice it in your blog entries and on the off chance that you have an email list – certainly let them realize you have a digital book available to be purchased.

2. On Amazon: You would self be able to distribute your book and sell it on Amazon effectively.

3. On ClickBank: ClickBank is an exceptionally famous online retailer for computerized items so selling your digital book on this stage can enable you to contact a wide group of spectators.

4. Set up for deals: Figure out how you will acknowledge installments and convey the digital book to your clients. You can do this effectively through a help like SendOwl (in case you're selling through your blog). Or on the other hand you can sell through Amazon or ClickBank as referenced previously.

You can likewise do your own arrangement, and acknowledge installments through a help like Paypal or Stripe and convey the digital books by means of email once you get an installment.

Do what is the most straightforward for you.

5. Advance your digital book: You have to get the word out about your digital book. Elevate your digital book to your email list, on Pinterest, on applicable Facebook gatherings and anyplace else that would be important. Try not to be modest to tell individuals you have something available to be purchased.

3. Online Courses

The subsequent stage up from digital books is making and selling on the web courses. Indeed, regularly bloggers will make a digital book and after that develop a similar theme in their online course.

Like digital books, you can make an online course about practically any point. Obviously, it ought to be a subject that individuals need to find out about and one you know a great deal about. At any rate enough to show a course.

A few thoughts… on the off chance that you have a nourishment blog, you can do a seminar on plans. On the off chance that you run a design blog, you could sell a seminar on style tips. In the event that you expound on connections, you could sell a seminar on the best way to oversee long separation connections.

You can sell your courses at more significant expense point than digital books yet the value you pick will truly rely upon the profundity of your course, your skill and how well your crowd definitely knows you.

I've seen short courses for $29, some for $47 and have likewise observed significant level specialists sell for $997. Research different courses in your specialty to perceive what the normal value point is.

Try not to overrate it yet don't undersell yourself either. Test a couple of costs and see what works best for you.

1. Pick a theme: Your course ought to be about a subject you can assist your group of spectators with. On the off chance that there's a battle or an issue that surfaces consistently, address it by making a course about.

2. Make your substance: Once your theme's set up, do the diligent work of arranging and making your course. There are numerous configurations to convey a course in yet most are normally a combo of recordings, slideshows and content.

Choose how you will convey data and make content in like manner.

You needn't bother with any extravagant hardware to begin. You can compose your contents in Google Docs and record your vides on your telephone (however utilize a tripod). Simply pick a peaceful spot and start making.

3. Make sense of where to sell: There are numerous approaches to sell a course on the web. A portion of your choices are:

>] All alone webpage: You can have your seminar all alone site

>] On Udemy (or other comparable destinations)

>] On Teachable (or other comparable stages.

>] Where you sell your course will likewise rely upon its intricacy. Stages like Teachable make it simple to make a course substantial on recordings and slideshows.

4. Set available to be purchased: Once individuals purchase your course, you will require an approach to convey the course to them.

At the extremely fundamental level, you can have your recordings on YouTube or Vimeo and convey it to your clients all alone site. To keep things basic, course makers regularly use stages, for example, Teachable or ClickFunnels. These stages help you have the course, yet additionally effectively acknowledge installments for your courses.

On the off chance that you've chosen to sell on Udemy to begin with, at that point the stage will manage you through the way toward setting up and selling a course through them.

5. Advance your course: Like everything else, in the event that you don't advance, nobody is going to know you

3 ONLINE TRADING FOREX/CRYPTO

How to make Money from Trading Online ?

In this section we will talk about Trading online by investing some money and then earn profit from it.

★Forex Trading

The foreign trade market is the world's most fluid market, with more than 5-trillion daily trading hands. The market is fluid 24-hours per day, 5-days every week, opening at night on Sunday during North American exchanging hours and shutting down at 5-pm on Friday evening during a similar time zone. On the off chance that you are an apprentice and simply dunking your toe into exchanging the forex markets, you ought to consider following the market and expanding your comprehension of why trade rates move before taking a chance with your well-deserved capital.

Find out About the Financial Markets

The monetary markets permit speculators, organizations, governments and national banks a spot to execute in an open market, trading their dangers to meet their money related needs. A corporate treasurer may need to trade benefits in Euros into dollars, similarly as a theorist accepts that the EUR/USD will rise. There are a great many reasons why trade rates and costs moved over a brief timeframe, creating commotion as members search at an ideal cost to enter or leave a position.

Before you start exchanging, you ought to find out about the various sorts of business sectors accessible to exchange, and which one you are most keen on following. Notwithstanding exchanging forex, you can likewise think about exchanging products, lists, and offers. The most ideal approach to find out about a market is to find out concerning why others trust it's moving and the various impetuses that may drive the cost or swapping scale a particular way. For instance, you may begin with searching for a style of investigation that is commonly given by trustworthy specialists, for example, Alpari. You will likely observe what kind of examination they offer and what sort of significant thoughts originate from the investigation they give. You can likewise glance through a specialist's instruction area and check whether they give data regarding why the business sectors move. Notwithstanding taking a gander at a dealer's training segment, you can check the business sectors for sites that attention on monetary markets instruction.

Figure out how to Do Your Own Analysis

There are two primary kinds of examination that forex brokers for the most part center around, which incorporate principal and specialized investigation. Crucial examination is the investigation of large scale occasions that will modify the course of a money pair. Specialized investigation is the investigation of value activity, including seeing force, patterns and inversion designs.

Principal Analysis

The essentials encompassing the forex markets depends on the financing costs markets of every one of the monetary forms that make up a conversion scale. For instance, in the event that you plan on exchanging the EUR/USD you need to have a measure of where loan costs are likely going in the Eurozone just as the United States. All in all, the more grounded an economy, the more probable the national bank is to raise loan fees, which help drive up market financing costs. The invert is likewise the situation for a more fragile economy where the national bank and market powers will probably drive loan fees lower.

The most ideal approach to decide whether an economy is solid is to have the option to assess nations budgetary data. This could incorporate their work data, their GDP, just as expansion data, for example, the shopper value record. Most trustworthy specialists will furnish you with a forex monetary schedule where you can perceive what market analysts anticipate that relative should history just as the real discharge. What is significant about basics is that each new snippet of data can change the heading of a swapping scale. On the off chance that the financial information is more noteworthy than or more terrible than anticipated, a swapping scale will move to mirror the new data.

Specialized Analysis

Specialized examination is the investigation of recorded costs. In spite of the fact that the past isn't constantly an indicator of things to come, various changes following explicit examinations can give you a check of where costs may move in the prospects. A portion of the more prominent specialized investigation studies incorporate assessing force. Force is the quickening or deceleration of value changes. In the event that you are keen on finding out about specialized investigation, you can take a gander at your merchant's instruction area, or pursue their specialized examination figures. There are additionally a few sites that will furnish you with training on various kinds of specialized investigation apparatuses. A portion of the more mainstream incorporate the MACD, the RSI, and Stochastics.

Discover great Broker

Your forex specialist encourages the execution of exchanges. While this is their most significant capacity, there are numerous highlights a representative like Alpari brings to the table which you ought to know about preceding storing assets at that merchant. In the first place, do some due industriousness. Look into audits by your forthcoming merchant and ensure there are no warnings. Misrepresentation cautions or issues with pulling back assets are the most significant. You likewise need to ensure there is proficient client care. You would prefer not to baffle yourself by finding an intermediary who won't respond to questions.

The following stage is to assess the stage. Does the dealer have training area or create specialized investigation conjectures? Furthermore, you need to ensure that your agent offers customers a money related schedule. Furthermore, you need to get some answers concerning the influence they give to customers. More elevated levels of edge will give you the choice to produce more income.

Start with a Demo Account

Most legitimate representatives will offer you genuine cash accounts just as showing accounts. A demo record is one where you are exchanging paper cash, not genuine capital. Most great exhibition records offer almost every one of the items that are accessible to exchange will a genuine cash account. The costs will probably be continuously or near ongoing. Moreover, you will approach the greater part of the training and anticipating data your specialist gives to genuine cash customers. When you sense that you're prepared for a genuine cash account you can change from a demo record to genuine assets.

Outline

There are a few stages you should take before you start executing in the forex advertise. You have to initially find out about the budgetary markets and the kind of data you can find out about preceding exchanging. Attempt to find out about both basic and specialized investigation. Discover a forex facilitate that you accept is dependable and gives a plenty of data. Ultimately, utilize a demo account before you start to chance genuine cash.

★ Forex Day Trading Risk Management

Every successful forex day trader manages their risk; it is one of, if not the, most crucial elements of ongoing profitability.

To start, you must keep your risk on each trade very small, and 1% or less is typical. This means if you have a $3,000 account, you shouldn't lose more than $30 on a single trade. That may seem small, but losses do add up, and even a good day-trading strategy will see strings of losses. Risk is managed using a stop-loss order, which will be discussed in the Scenario sections below.

Forex Day Trading Strategy

While a strategy can potentially have many components and can be analyzed for profitability in various ways, a strategy is often ranked based on its win-rate and risk/reward ratio.

Win Rate

Your win rate represents the number of trades you win out a given total number of trades. Say you win 55 out of 100 trades, your win rate is 55 percent. While it isn't required, having a win rate above 50 percent is ideal for most day traders, and 55 percent is acceptable and attainable.

Risk/Reward

Risk/reward signifies how much capital is being risked attaining a certain profit. If a trader loses 10 pips on losing trades but makes 15 on winning trades, she is making more on the winners than she's losing on losers. This means that even if the trader only wins 50% of her trades, she will be profitable. Therefore, making more on winning trades is also a strategic component for which many forex day traders strive.

A higher win rate for trades means more flexibility with your risk/reward, and a high risk/reward means your win rate can be lower and you'd still be profitable.

Hypothetical Scenario

Assume a trader has $5,000 in capital funds, and they have a decent win rate of 55% on their trades. They risk only 1% of their capital or $50 per trade. This is accomplished by using a stop-loss order. For this scenario, a stop-loss order is placed 5 pips away from the trade entry price, and a target is placed 8 pips away.

This means that the potential reward for each trade is 1.6 times greater than the risk (8/5). Remember, you want winners to be bigger than losers.

While trading a forex pair for two hours during an active time of day it's usually possible to make about five round turn trades (round turn includes entry and exit) using the above parameters. If there are 20 trading days in a month, the trader is making 100 trades, on average, in a month.

Trading Leverage

Forex brokers provide leverage up to 50:1 (more in some countries). For this example, assume the trader is using 30:1 leverage, as usually that is more than enough leverage for forex day traders. Since the trader has $5,000, and leverage is 30:1, the trader is able to take positions worth up to $150,000. Risk is still based on the original $5,000;

this keeps the risk limited to a small portion of the deposited capital.

Forex brokers often don't charge a commission, but rather increase the <u>spread between the bid and ask</u>, thus making it more difficult to day trade profitably. ECN brokers offer a very small spread, making it easier to trade profitably, but they typically charge about $2.50 for every $100,000 traded ($5 round turn).

Trading Currency Pairs

If you're day trading a currency pair like the GBP/USD, you can risk $50 on each trade, and each pip of movement is worth $10 with a standard lot (100,000 units worth of currency). Therefore you can take a position of one standard lot with a 5-pip stop-loss order, which will keep the risk of loss to $50 on the trade. That also means a winning trade is worth $80 (8 pips x $10).

This estimate can show how much a forex day trader could make in a month by executing 100 trades:

- 55 trades were profitable: 55 x $80 = $4,400
- 45 trades were losers: 45 x ($50) = ($2,250)

Gross profit is $4,400 - $2,250 = $2,150 if no commissions (win rate would likely be lower though)

Net profit is $2,150 - $500 = $1, 650 if using a commission broker (win rate would like be higher though)

Assuming a net profit of $1,650, the return on the account for the month is 33 percent ($1,650/$5,000). This may seem very high, and it is a very good return. See Refinements below to see how this return may be affected.

Slippage Larger Than Expected Loss

It won't always be possible to find five good day trades each day, especially when the market is moving very slowly for extended periods.

Slippage is an inevitable part of trading. It results in a larger loss than expected, even when using a stop-loss order. It's common in very fast-moving markets.

To account for slippage in the calculation of your potential profit, reduce the net profit by 10% (this is a high estimate for slippage, assuming you avoid holding through major economic data releases). This would reduce the net profit potential generated by your $5,000 trading capital to $1,485 per month.

You can adjust the scenario above based on your typical stop loss and target, capital, slippage, win rate, position size, and commission parameters.

To Cover UP:-

This simple risk-controlled strategy indicates that with a 55% win rate, and making more on winners than you lose on losing trades, it's possible to attain returns north of 20% per month with forex day trading. Most traders shouldn't expect to make this much; while it sounds simple, in reality, it's more difficult.

Even so, with a decent win rate and risk/reward ratio, a dedicated forex day trader with a decent strategy can make between 5% and 15% a month thanks to leverage. Also remember, you don't need much capital to get started; $500 to $1,000 is usually enough.

How to Read a Forex Quote

Currencies are always quoted in pairs, such as GBP/USD or USD/JPY. The reason they are quoted in pairs is because, in every foreign exchange transaction, you are simultaneously buying one currency and selling another.

Here is an example of a foreign exchange rate for the British pound versus the U.S. dollar:

GBP / USD = 1.32448

(Base Currency)   (Quote Currency)

The first listed currency to the left of the slash ("/") is known as the **base currency** (in this example, the British pound), while the second one on the right is called the **counter or quote currency** (in this example, the U.S. dollar).When buying, the exchange rate tells you how much you have to pay in units of the quote currency to buy **ONE unit of the base currency**. In the example above, you have to pay 1.51258 U.S. dollars to buy 1 British pound. When selling, the exchange rate tells you how many units of the quote currency you get for selling **ONE unit of the base currency**. In the example above, you will receive 1.51258 U.S. dollars when you sell 1 British pound.

The base currency is the "basis" for the buy or the sell.

If you buy EUR/USD this simply means that you are buying the base currency and simultaneously selling the quote currency. In caveman talk, "buy EUR, sell USD." You would *buy* the pair if you believe the base currency will appreciate (gain value) relative to the quote currency.

You would *sell* the pair if you think the base currency will depreciate (lose value) relative to the quote currency.

Long/Short

First, you should determine whether you want
to **buy** or **sell**. If you want to buy (which actually means buy the base currency and sell the quote currency), you want the base currency to rise in value and then you would sell it back at a higher price.
In trader talk, this is called "going long" or taking a "long position." Just remember: **long = buy.**
If you want to sell (which actually means sell the base currency and buy the quote currency), you want the base currency to fall in value and then you would buy it back at a lower price. This is called "going short" or taking a "short position". Just remember: **short = sell.**

The Bid, Ask and Spread

All forex quotes are quoted with two prices:
the **bid** and **ask**. In general, the **bid** is lower than the **ask** price. The **bid** is the price at which your broker is willing to *buy* the base currency in exchange for the quote currency.
This means the bid is the best available price at which you (the trader) will sell to the market. If you want to sell something, the broker will buy it from you at the bid price.
The **ask** is the price at which your broker will *sell* the base currency in exchange for the quote currency.
This means the ask price is the best available price at which you will buy from the market. Another word for ask is the **offer price.** If you want to buy something, the broker will sell (or offer) it to you at the ask price.
The difference between the bid and the ask price is known as the **SPREAD**.

On the EUR/USD quote above, the bid price is 1.34568 and the ask price is 1.34588. Look at how this broker makes it so easy for you to trade away your money.

If you want to sell EUR, you click "Sell" and you will sell euros at 1.34568.If you want to buy EUR, you click "Buy" and you will buy euros at 1.34588.

★STOCK MARKET

The stock exchange, or values showcase as it is likewise known, is one of the world's most prevalent and effectively exchanged budgetary markets. It's additionally a spot where numerous individuals go to attempt to profit, both rapidly and over the long haul. There are numerous approaches to profit in the financial exchange, utilizing both conventional strategies and some increasingly imaginative techniques.

What Are Stocks?

Responsibility for in fact speaks to the proprietorship, or if nothing else halfway possession, of organizations. Proprietors of stocks in many nations have a lawful right to cast a ballot at organization investors' gatherings and will get a notice when the gatherings are held. After offers are given by organizations, they can be (and typically are) exchanged progressively on the optional market.

There are a few different ways to profit with the buy, possession and closeout of stock in the financial exchange:

Development Stocks

Stocks whose organizations are relied upon to encounter solid development are known as development stocks. One of the fundamental ways brokers can profit with them is holding their offers until they increment in cost, and after that offering them to take a benefit (also called a capital addition). Some of the time, share costs will change uncontrollably in unpredictable markets, offering dealers chances to purchase, sell and take benefits quickly.

Initial public offering

At the point when organizations first issue offers to general society, they hold beginning open contributions (IPOs) to permit first buy rights to potential purchasers. A few IPOs are intently viewed and vigorously exchanged. That is on the grounds that stock costs from promising new organizations can be offered up rapidly from low levels to exceptionally significant levels in a brief timeframe. This produces open doors for snappy and once in a while soak profits.

Value Stocks

As the name proposes, esteem stocks are those that are underestimated by the market, displaying a decent can foresee potential purchasers. Worth contributing can require intensive examination of an organization's budget reports to comprehend its monetary wellbeing and future potential, yet this might merit the exertion.

Acclaimed financial specialist Warren Buffett is one surely understood advocate of significant worth contributing. Roused by the worth contributing procedures of contributing theoretician Benjamin Graham, Buffett had the option to store up a fortune searching out underestimated stocks over a time of quite a while. Graham accepted that stocks spoke to a decent arrangement when they were estimated at 66% or less of their "natural" value.

Income Stocks

Holding salary stocks is a conventional method to profit in the financial exchange. Loads of organizations that acquire strong incomes regularly pay profits, more often than not on a quarterly premise, to investors. Stocks that pay generally higher profits, or salary stocks, can habitually profit for their proprietors. Be that as it may, dealers may frequently need to gather a lot of such stocks to get huge profit installments.

Stock Funds

Holding common assets, or trade exchanged assets, is another way that merchants can make cash on stocks. A reserve is comprised of a gathering of money related resources, frequently stocks, that are packaged all together security. Shared assets regularly require least buy sums and are not exchanged during business sector hours.

Trade exchanged assets are like shared assets, however are exchanged during business sector hours as though they were individual stocks and can be purchased and sold in littler additions than common assets. Both common assets and trade exchanged subsidizes that hold stocks frequently pay out profits from their possessions on a standard basis

Investment opportunities And Futures

The alternatives and fates markets are in fact not part of the securities exchanges, yet they can give great chances to profiting with stocks.

In alternatives exchanging, merchants can get the choice to purchase or sell a stock at a predetermined cost at a future lapse date. In the event that the securities exchange's cost is higher or lower than the choice's predefined strike cost at its termination date, at that point the holder of the choice can practice their purchasing or selling right and pocket the distinction between the two costs. Alternatives can likewise be purchased or sold on the auxiliary market before the termination date. Additionally, prospects agreements are sold for certain significant stock files and some individual stocks.

Prospects agreements are sold at an expected future cost for the list or stock. The agreements for the most part terminate four times each year, once close to the finish of each quarter. In the event that the stock or record worth is higher than the fates cost at termination, the purchaser of the agreement can take a benefit. On the off chance that the worth is lower, the vender of the agreement takes a profit.

Preferred Stock Vs. Common Stock

Stocks are generally given in two kinds: favored stock and normal stock. Normal investors, as referenced above, are given democratic rights. Favored investors don't have casting a ballot rights. In any case, favored stock more often than not gets higher profit installments than normal stock and has more noteworthy assurances of reimbursement should the organization default on some loans.

Some favored offers are likewise convertible into regular offers. These offers can be changed over at a predefined proportion. In the event that the cost of the convertible favored offers is lower than the cost of basic offers after the change rate is applied, the favored offers can be traded for normal offers at a benefit to the shareholder.

Short-Selling

Short-selling a stock is another basic method for profiting with stocks. While brokers frequently consider purchasing, or going "long," on stocks they think will ascend in an incentive as a manner to pick up cash, short-selling adopts the contrary strategy.

Short merchants obtain shares, ordinarily from their intermediary, so as to sell, or "short," stocks they think will fall in worth. After the offers fall in value, they repurchase them and return them to the moneylender. They pocket the distinction in the cost at which they sold the offers and the lower cost at which they got them back.

Stock Splits

Stock parts can on occasion be endorsed by organization sheets and investors. At the point when a stock split happens, the investor is conceded a different number of extra offers for each offer held, in proportions of 2-to-1, 3-to at least 1. The estimation of each offer is separated in a comparing way. Yet, when a split happens, the investor's potential future property of the organization, and comparing riches, might be helped significantly.

Summary

There are an assortment of approaches to profit in the securities exchange, and subsequently it is where numerous dealers go to look for formation of riches. Stocks, similar to any money related exchanging, can include potential dangers and misfortunes. Be that as it may, merchants may improve their odds by getting comfortable with the numerous roads wherein to utilize the financial exchange furthering their potential benefit.

Any sentiments, news, look into, examinations, costs, other data, or connections to outsider locales are given as general market critique and don't comprise venture counsel. FXCM won't acknowledge risk for any misfortune or harm including, without constraint, to any loss of benefit which may emerge legitimately or in a roundabout way from utilization of or dependence on such data.

★ Bitcoin

So you want to get your hands on some free bitcoin, eh? By now, you might have heard of how you can make money with bitcoin, magic internet money and digital currency that can be traded or used to make purchases. This digital money uses encryption to make safe and secure transactions instantly from anywhere in the world. Not regulated by any bank, government or Federal Reserve, this open network is managed by the users and investors themselves. Here is our guide to earning real money with bitcoin in 2019.

Contrary to people's knowledge, getting bitcoin is easy, there are a number of ways to earn bitcoin online- some more popular than the others. There are methods that involve a minimal effort with the minimal return and others more lucrative that requires you to have better expertise in the industry.

Below are some of the most famous ways to make money with bitcoin.

1.Mining bitcoin

No, you don't have to raise the ground to get bitcoin. Not in that sense anyway.

So, why do you call it mining? Similar to gold miners, bitcoin miners have to bring out the gold, in this case, bitcoin into the surface.

Did you dare to ask how? While paper money has a government, who prints and distributes it, Bitcoin has miners who use special software to solve math problems and are issued with bitcoin in exchange. This system is what makes the Bitcoin network go round.

Mining Bitcoin used to be relatively simple, and the earliest miners were able to mine thousands of Bitcoin using their home computers. However, in today's very competitive and volatile market, miners buy expensive computer parts, that the high street customer has little access to, required for more processing power in order to mine more difficult algorithms. Since this is a race who can solve blocks faster, miners team up in what we call mining pools where they combine their processing power in order to solve each transaction first. The reward mostly comes from several miners' fees, is then split up by members of the pool.

Remember that bitcoin mining is not as profitable as it used to and many are claiming it to be the end of profitable mining.

The future of mining in 2019 will depend on the price of Bitcoin. If the price goes up, mining will continue to evolve and the number of miners will increase. If the price goes down, miners will gradually disappear.an excerpt from 2miners' blog
It presents new miners with new challenges and also unique opportunities to come into the market when everyone else is leaving and then the price of bitcoin will go up. It all depends on your ability to analyze the market and correctly predict future changes.

instructions to profit with bitcoin , One of the most well known methods for how to benefit from Bitcoin will be Bitcoin mining. There can be two types of mining – your own, own mining or cloud mining.

In the event that you need to mine separately (which means, with your mining rig), it probably won't be the most ideal method for how to profit with Bitcoin. Bitcoin is viewed as one of the harder cryptographic forms of money to mine since it's a subject of standard achievement and many individuals need to pitch into the publicity, yet there's restricted stockpile of it. A solitary apparatus, in the same class as it could be, might battle to create noteworthy benefits, particularly when you consider the power and support costs.

Cloud mining, in any case, has turned out to be prominent in the course of the most recent couple of years. It's an incredible elective with regards to mining since you don't have to purchase any equipment or programming, collect or even DO anything – you should simply pay a one-time expense for an agreement and that is it! For the most part, toward the finish of consistently, you'll get your income.

The sum will be founded on your arrangement of decision and the power bill at the office that the cloud mining administration depends on.

Generally speaking, digital currency mining is a prevalent strategy for individuals looking on the most proficient method to profit with Bitcoin. It requires some learning and aptitude in the field to have the option to perform it effectively (particularly on the off chance that you need to manufacture your apparatus), however the exertion is unquestionably worth the outcomes.

2. Bitcoin Faucets

If you don't mind looking at a few ads and answering surveys, you can visit a bitcoin faucet website. Generally, these websites generate revenue from advertisements placed on their pages. Those who visit their site and answer short questions or captchas will be paid from the small portion of their revenue. You can readily check one of the most popular faucet sites here: earn.com.

3. Pay To Click (PTC) Websites

There are several websites that will pay you in bitcoin if you watch an ad or click to a certain page containing ads. If you are ad immune and want to make quick crypto buck–this can be a good idea. Bear in mind, to make any significant money is still very hard work and a rather tedious task. BTC4ADS pays around 100 satoshis (0.00000100 ฿) and Coinadder pays around 25 satoshis per click.

4. Doing Micro Jobs

Much like Microworkers and Cloudfactory, which pay you a small fee to complete very simple tasks like watching a YouTube video or completing someone's survey, there are several micro working sites that will pay you in bitcoin. Bitcoinget is the major player in this market which will pay you around 20,000 satoshis per task while there are several others like Cointasker that will pay you a slightly lower sum.

5. Writing about bitcoin

Cryptocurrency, in general, is a new niche and there is a scarcity of writers who genuinely know this niche. This means the market is flooded with newbie copywriters who simply rehash the content that contributes to the deterioration of quality. However, if you really know this niche and you have decent writing skills, you can actually make money.

CCN, Blockchain Aliens are among several websites that pay you for writing about bitcoin. You can also find a lot of related jobs freelance websites like upwork and freelancer.com

6. Help others, get tipped in bitcoin

You can also get tipped in bitcoin by helping other people. One of the most notable platform to do so is bitfortip, which tips bitcoin as an incentive for helping people. Bitcoin is a new technology and there are people who are genuinely passionate about it and excited about what is to follow so incentives like this help to build a positive vibe around the community and also help people solve their problems.

7. Gambling bitcoin

Though its not advisable to anyone, if you are self-aware enough, the bitcoin gambling market can still be a good source of income. Just like any form of gambling, the people in general always lose and the casinos always win but since bitcoin gambling is a very little heard of the term, you can get huge bonus for joining or even several rounds of your stake to start with. Sites like Bitstarz and mbit are major players in Crypto gambling business.

8. Buying and Holding

Start with creating a wallet to keep your bitcoin safe. There are many places that allow you to do so. Paxful, for example, provides a free digital wallet whenever you sign up for an account. This is the easiest way if you are planning on buying and holding bitcoin. Make sure that the website you're using is a safe and reliable one. Investing in Bitcoin is a waiting game of its value to rise. This lets you decide when is a good time to buy or sell. There are several factors that contribute to how bitcoin is valued and you never know what will trigger the next bear market.

"Hodl", a term the Bitcoin community whenever they are holding their coin with the belief their coin will be profitable one day. The slang word earned the backronym "Hold On for Dear Life" in the cryptocurrency space.

Note that this method can be tricky so don't take anyone's advice about it. Research and learn about Bitcoin and come up to your own conclusion.

9. Running a signature campaign in Bitcoin Talk forum

Bitcointalk is one of the oldest bitcoin forum set up by Satoshi Nakamoto himself. This is probably the most popular forum in crypto sphere and used by millions of people. If you are an avid follower of the forum and you have racked up some authority from consistent posting, then your posts of bitcointalk will have a sponsored signature and you'll get paid by sponsors for every post you make on the forum.

According to Steemit, you can easily make a bit of coin doing simple forum posting – for example, a full member can earn 0.0003 btc per post

10. Bitcoin Trading

There is potential to make big money trading bitcoin. Unlike buying and holding, trading bitcoin means you buy at a low price and sell them back at a higher price. This requires practice and knowledge of the market and to some extent a crystal ball. Given that the cryptocurrency market is extremely volatile, this method can be very risky.

"There is money in Arbitrage"
The volatile nature of the market, however, gives rise to the opportunities for arbitrage. Arbitrage–as per Investopedia is the simultaneous buying and selling of securities, currency, or commodities in different markets or

in derivative forms in order to take advantage of differing prices for the same asset.

There are several reasons why bitcoin arbitrage takes place, Market demands, the difference in the quality of the markets and diversity in client behaviors to name a few. If you have a good knowledge of the market and you can keep surveillance over multiple exchanges spanning over multiple countries, there is a good chance of making a big profit margin.

If you have at least some technical knowledge, you can also profit from using arbitrage bots.

Profit Strategy using bitcoin bots arbitrage
Day trading has a good profit margin if done correctly
Though bitcoin is getting less volatile by day, we should not forget that its still early adoption years and there was price fluctuations of more than 3% in a single minute as early as April 2018. Day trading has a lower risk than say "hodling" but also lower rewards unless you are investing heavily. But if you are prepared to do your research on the bitcoin market and rules of economics in general, you can come up with your own strategies to profit from day trading without sacrificing too much.

11. Accepting Bitcoin as a means of payment

Bitcoin is, after all, a digital currency. So why not sell goods or services in exchange for bitcoin. This gives you the freedom to sell anything to anyone without going through any banks or financial institutions that may prevent you to do so. If you are already selling, why not accept bitcoin as payment. As a matter of fact, there is a massive list of businesses that are already accepting bitcoin.

These are some ways in which you can earn money with bitcoin. If you choose to mine or invest, it is important to do as much research as possible and be prepared for all possible outcomes.

12. Lending bitcoin

The decentralized nature of bitcoin and other cryptocurrencies make it simpler to make transactions without needing authorities to validate it. In such a case, you can also loan bitcoin to potential loaners at a certain interest rate. It is also a very good alternative to "hodling" as you are actually making use of the wealth rather than keep it unmoved and it's better for the economy in general. Several lend-and-borrow platforms like Unchained Capital, Bitbond and BTCpop allow you to lend your bitcoin for interest rate up to 15%.

Bear in mind that this is still a new market and there are hustlers who may try to cheat you. Always choose trustworthy platforms and loaners while making your investments.

13. Binary Trading with bitcoin

Binary trading's have existed in the financial world for a very long time and did not take long enough to make a journey for that financial scheme to migrate to the crypto world. Binary—as the name suggests has just two options, a trader purchases an option and at the expiration time, the trader either is either "in the money" or "out of the money". In its true essence, its not too much further from gambling or Russian roulette.

All you have to do is make an investment on an option. Say there are two options to invest– for the bitcoin price of $3000 now (at 10 AM), you can either invest in the price will be more than $3000 by 6 PM or the price will be less than $3000 by 6 PM. If at 5 PM the bitcoin is indeed higher than $3000, you earn the payout of certain payout percentage of your investment, if it's lower, you lose your investment. Another option is to "put" if you think the price of BTC will go down. If the price at the expiration time is lower than the original price, you earn the option's payout.

Remember its plain gambling and nothing to do with intricacies of bitcoin or other cryptos in any way. Nonetheless, its still a way to make money with bitcoin though its highly inadvisable.

14. Make money with Bitcoin Affiliates

Affiliate marketing works when you generate sales leads for a product or a service and the organization offering a product or service pays you certain commission for bringing in potential consumers who would otherwise not have been interested.

Usually, these 3 steps allow you to set up your own affiliate business for passive income:

Sign up for the affiliate program as an affiliate marketer. When you are accepted as a marketer, you will receive a unique URL that has a link to their product or service but also has a unique identifier which means they keep a record of who sent them there.

You then share that link on any web or social media platform(Website, Facebook, Twitter etc.) When someone comes to visit the website through your link and makes a purchase, you get a certain percentage as your affiliate fee. We at Paxful also have an amazing affiliate program where you get paid 50% of the bitcoin escrow fee from your direct affiliate and 10% of the escrow fee from the affiliates made by your affiliates.

15. Being a Master node

Bitcoin is usually used as an umbrella term for all the cryptocurrencies and though experts would say the return for being a bitcoin master node is not all that profitable, you can still serve as a master node for several other cryptocurrencies and get a reward for your service to the blockchain.

Master node is a dedicated node that keeps track of blockchain in real-time. Much like bitcoin full nodes, they are always up and running.

In addition to saving, validating and announcing valid transactions to other nodes, master nodes also perform other tasks with the blockchain including ensuring smooth protocol operations, governing voting events etc Next to validating, saving and broadcasting transactions, master nodes sometimes also facilitate other events on the blockchain-dependent on their nature, such as governing voting events etc. For their dedicated service, they are heavily incentivized. It typically depends on the type of cryptocurrency but Dash, PIVX, Blocknet, Stakenet and Zcoin are the 5 major coins that have the best incentives for a master node.

Tips for making more profit with bitcoin

Needed to say, here are a few tips before you start earning money through bitcoin.

Like having physical cash, keep your bitcoin safe and keep your bitcoin wallet safe. This may mean enabling your Google 2FA, backing up your device or keeping your antivirus updated. There are a lot of digital threats waiting for you.

The industry is prone to fluctuations. This can be a good thing when you stay on top of it and learn the risk that comes with it.

Keep in mind that there is no free Bitcoin. Although there are several methods to earn from it. With the market always growing, there will always be a demand in expertise or a new product that will develop with time.

More about Bitcoin:-

Bitcoin, as a digital currency, has been dependent upon standard discussion for a long while now. Individuals investigate its past and theorize about its future for a wide assortment of reasons – a few people need to know the historical backdrop of cryptographic forms of money, others are interested about conceivable venture openings. Whatever your explanation would be, in this guide we'll discuss various methods for how to profit with Bitcoin.

We'll discuss the various methods for how to benefit from Bitcoin – yet most importantly, we'll contemplate on why Bitcoin is so prominent in any case. At that point, when we comprehend the history (or if nothing else its overly short form) of this present digital currency's development and ascend to control, we will investigate its benefitting openings.

ˌ The Short Version of Bitcoin History

ˌ The Fall of Bitcoin

ˌ How to profit with Bitcoin?

ˌ Buying Bitcoin

ˌ Investing

The Short Version of Bitcoin History

Bitcoin was made in 2009 by somebody (or some gathering of individuals) known by the nom de plume Satoshi Nakamoto. At the time that it came around, no one had even known about digital currencies, not to mention experienced one.

Bitcoins newborn child and high school years were truly harsh – it neglected to increase noteworthy footing and consideration, despite the fact that its costs varied for what (around then) appeared to be a considerable amount. Nobody was all the while considering how to profit with Bitcoin.

At last, toward the start of 2017 Bitcoin broke the benchmark of $1000. In simply a question of a year, it figured out how to nearly come to the $20,000 checkmark. Obviously, this was tremendous – everyone either remained with their jawlines arriving at the floor or emptied all that they had into Bitcoin – it appeared to be a relentless power that continued expanding its energy each and every day. In the event that you've as of late checked the Bitcoin value graphs, in any case, you realize that things went in a new direction.

The Fall of Bitcoin

Toward the start of 2018, Bitcoin's cost was around $11,000, at that point arrived at a stunning low of nearly $6000. At the hour of composing this guide, Bitcoin is at present worth $6400. So… How to profit with Bitcoin?

What caused an accident of this greatness? Indeed, there are numerous theories.

Individuals who frequently see how to profit with cryptographic money will presumably realize what the Bitcoin value diagram resembles:

step by step instructions to profit with bitcoin - diagram

Does it, maybe, help you to remember something? A… tooth, possibly?

This sort of outline is known as a "shark tooth" graph. It implies that a digital currency's (for this situation – Bitcoin's) value rose and fell so quick that the way it took on the diagram looks like a sharp shark tooth.

This is likewise called a "burst bubble". A celebrated financial specialist was even cited saying that Bitcoin was the "greatest air pocket burst ever". Purposes for this are estimated to be the developed publicity, absence of help for the blockchain, advertise controls and many, some more.

Whatever the case may be, clearly if nothing else, Bitcoin took a colossal jump from which it is as of now attempting to recoup. Anyone seeing how to profit with Bitcoin ought to presumably remember these things.

How to profit with Bitcoin?

So since you know a few things about the ascent and fall of Bitcoin, we can at long last move into the lucrative techniques.

There are many techniques to profit with the assistance of Bitcoin, however in this guide, I'll spread only the fundamental ones – in the event that I needed to show them all, this guide would be in any event 300 pages in length.

The rundown isn't formed in a particular request. A few techniques work better (or quicker) than others, however – for the most part – it relies upon the individual.

Buying Bitcoin

No, I'm not kidding.

There are gigantic gatherings of individuals who "contribute" into Bitcoin by essentially getting it. This is a dangerous strategy, obviously, yet most likely the least difficult one to perform.

There are two or three kinds of such speculators. A few people simply purchase a specific amount of the coin and forget about it for a year… or ten. These individuals typically have no genuine expectation to benefit present moment – they regularly put stock in the effective eventual fate of digital forms of money and expectation that their venture currently will one day present to them a ten times benefit.

Another kind of Bitcoin financial specialists are the individuals who do heaps of research, read the majority of the accessible expectations on the most proficient method to profit with digital currency and go through weeks breaking down information and insights. These individuals will in general have a quite certain time span as a main priority – more often than not, they are hoping to contribute present moment and simply need to realize when to do it. Additionally, these ventures will in general be littler when contrasted with the long haul ones – all things considered, individuals contribute having done a huge amount of research previously, yet in the event that their speculation fizzles, they could simply proceed onward to whenever outline.

In case you're contemplating how to profit with Bitcoin or how to profit with cryptographic money when all is said in done, purchasing Bitcoin can be an extraordinary starter – or a grievous one. It can profit genuine quick or might drive you to the edge of obligation. Everything relies upon one single factor – the measure of research you've done already.

Investing

What's more, no, not the purchasing bitcoin-and afterward selling-it sort of contributing.

There are many decisions you have with regards to putting resources into Bitcoin. You could profit with Bitcoin by putting resources into new businesses, organizations, stocks or even blockchain advancement itself.

Blockchain-based new businesses are an exceptionally famous decision with regards to putting resources into a digital currency related field. Effectively, some eminent new companies have made it into the standard achievement (for example Daring's Basic Attention Token). You would need to do some uncovering and locate the following best thing, however on the off chance that you'd be correct and put resources into the startup while it's still in its beginning of earliest stages, you may very well cashed in big and develop your benefits to the rooftop.

Organizations that manage Bitcoin or blockchain advancement (or research) are additionally a decent choice for speculations. You'd need to investigate their information – White Paper, their objectives and hard working attitudes, results, insights, and so on., and if their general view appears to be appealing, you could consider putting resources into their activities or the organization itself.

You ought to be cautious with ventures, however – particularly with regards to digital forms of money. Its a well known fact that the cryptographic money market is a truly capricious spot. Continuously get your work done and inquire about the articles that you intend to put into, or else the topic of "how to profit with Bitcoin?" may transform into "how to escape obligation (no Bitcoin)?".

★ **Cryptocurrency**

You will adapt precisely how to make cash exchanging altcoins
2017 was a major year for digital currency, however it's still early days.
… And now everybody's searching for the following Bitcoin.

To enable you to find precisely how to make cash exchanging altcoins – without taking a chance with your entire speculation.

1. What Are Altcoins?

Altcoins are essentially simply some other cryptographic money separated from Bitcoin. Presently while Bitcoin is the most notable cryptographic money, there's still more than 2,000 altcoins available – and the greater part of them aren't anyplace close as well known.
Also, more alternatives = increasingly potential exchanging benefits.
Here's some ongoing instances of digital forms of money that have expanded by 1,000+ percent in just 24 hours…
Be that as it may, this isn't just about profiting!
Altcoins offer heaps of advantages – as you you'll find underneath…

2. 7 Reasons Why You Should Learn How To Make Money Trading Altcoins

1 You needn't bother with a great deal of cash.
Regardless of whether you start off contributing just $100, you can in any case make good comes back with the intensity of self multiplying dividends. Which leads me to my next point…

2 The profits are absurd.
100% gains in a day? 1,000% in a month? When you figure out how to make cash exchanging altcoins, these sorts of increases are entirely

achieveable – which overwhelms the profits you'll
see on most customary ventures.

3 Cryptocurrency is what's to come.

While there might be an air pocket at the present
time, digital money is an amazingly troublesome
innovation. That is to say, digital currency could
actually change the eventual fate of cash!
Protection, online security, obscurity, everyday
installments – these are only a couple of the ways
altcoins could change our reality. Exchanging
digital currency resembles picking the following
Apple, Amazon or Tesla!

4 Altcoins are blasting at the present time

. Since the brilliant ascent of Bitcoin, there will
never be been a superior time to put resources
into cryptographic forms of money. What's more,
I completely expect altcoin exchanging to blast in
2018.

5 It's enjoyable.

The cosmic highs. The sensational lows. The
1,000% increases… Is there much else fun than
the rush of riding the cryptographic money wave?
Evidently, there's a LOT of hazard with regards to
altcoins – yet that is a piece of the ride. Simply
make sure to contribute capably.

6 It's anything but difficult to begin.

It may take two or three days to get confirmed on
Coinbase (where a great many people purchase
their Bitcoin) – however once you're in, you're in.

You needn't bother with any understanding, capabilities or huge cash to get included.

3. Instructions to Make Money Trading Altcoins.

A little tip:
Take as much time as necessary and don't race through the means beneath!
It's essential to look into your altcoins throroughly, comprehend the dangers and think cautiously before you place any exchanges.

Presently immediately, here's the means by which to make cash exchanging altcoins in 7 basic advances.

1. Sign Up To Coinbase.

Before you can start exchanging altcoins, you have to purchase Bitcoin.
A great many people get their Bitcoin from Coinbase – it's a snappy, simple approach to get it on the web.

2. Move Your Money To An Exchange.

You can exchange altcoins at trades – two of the most prevalent are Bittrex and Binance. Trades are the place most major altcoins are recorded – they're just a spot where you can purchase and sell crypto on the web, kinda like eBay for cryptographic money!

3. Waitlist Your Altcoins.

Presently I realize what you're thinking...
When there's a great many altcoins to look over, how would you realize which is ideal? By and by, I'd suggest searching for a long haul altcoin that you wouldn't see any problems with holding for a half year or more – just in the event that the market changes.

4. Contribute.

Keep in mind: costs are unpredictable to the point that they can change from moment to minute by a couple of percent...
So I'd suggest hanging tight for a plunge in the market before you put resources into your top pick. These plunges will in general happen at regular intervals in the middle of high development spurts.
You can watch out for the most recent digital currency costs

5. Screen Your Gains.

Trades like Bittrex or Binance make it simple to follow your benefits/misfortunes.
Also, when costs are fluctuating so quickly, it gets a brief period devouring to continually figure costs.
Rather, introduce the Blockfolio application. Blockfolio refreshes your digital currency portfolio every time you open it – and it's really simple to utilize as well.

6. Sell Up When You're Ready.

So how would you realize when you're prepared to sell?

Set benefit targets – and when you hit them, sell out.

At the point when you're figuring out how to make cash exchanging altcoins, it's anything but difficult to become overly enthusiastic with voracity. Be that as it may, don't let occur! Since when costs are so unstable, if something goes up, it'll in all likelihood shoot down as well. What's more, this typically occurs all of a sudden! So sell up and get out when you hit your benefit limits.

Note: a great many people exchange their altcoins over into BTC when they're prepared to sell out.

7. Money Out.

Keep in mind: You haven't made anything until you money out. Of course, those 100% increases are extraordinary... In any case, they don't mean anything until the cash is in your bank!

So just move your parity back to Coinbase – and afterward money them out into your ledger. It may take two or three days for the cash to come through.

4. Data Is Everything.

At the point when you're figuring out how to make cash exchanging altcoins, you can take a brazen easy route!

... You see, I'm no exchange examiner.

... I don't try to be one.

... And I'm ridiculous horrendous at maths!

Be that as it may, you don't have to understand diagrams or ace numbers to figure out how to make cash exchanging altcoins.
All you need is the capacity to inquire about.
Since data = benefits. Each time there's another update, official statement or enormous declaration, you'll find that the costs of altcoins change pretty quickly. So join some Facebook gatherings. Peruse some ICO white papers. Sweep through the most recent digital currency news on Reddit.

What's more, discover all that you can about your ventures.

8. Data Pays Off.

As of late, I made generally 90% on Bitcoin Cash the day preceding it was recorded on Coinbase... In any case, I had no aim of selling up until I got a tip off that Bitcoin Cash was going to crash! Soon after, heaps of venders dumped it in a major frenzy sell.

Quick forward 24 hours and Bitcoin Cash has dropped by 70%! Perceive how significant data is presently?

Proven Altcoin Trading Strategies

1. Slow, Compound Interest Gains.

On the off chance that you don't extravagant exchanging the high hazard, unstable altcoins – don't stress!
Rather, just spotlight on making a little rate increase regular. 10% a day may appear to be

moderate, however it develops speedy with accumulated dividends.

For instance, in the event that you made 10% premium every day for 25 days, you'd twofold your venture! Test out what you could gain with progressive accrual here.

What's more, that is very feasible with altcoins yet it does a ton of training and specialized learning.

2. HODL.

Discover a cryptographic money you can stay with longterm and essentially hold it.

It's basic AF. In any case, it likewise has exactly the intended effect!

On the off chance that you'd held Bitcoin since January 2017, you would have made a fortune. Furthermore, in the event that you put resources into a legitimate altcoin that has an extraordinary future, at that point the circumstance is the same.

Need a few hints? Look at my rundown of the best cryptographic forms of money to put resources into for 2018.

3. Pursue The Hype.

With regards to exchanging altcoins, your opposition isn't very keen.

You're not contending with Wall Street… Or banks… Or especially refined programming.

When it comes to altcoins, you're basically simply exchanging a market brimming with regular person's hoping to acquire a speedy buck.

So while Bitcoin is being savaged by Wall Street, altcoins haven't hit the standard market. They're just facilitated on trades – which means you're not

going up against numerous star level merchants…
yet!

4. Exchanging Altcoins Comes With A Lot Of Risk.

With enormous returns comes greater duties!

What's more, with regards to figuring out how to make cash exchanging altcoins, a tremendous piece of the game is dealing with the potential dangers.

Keep in mind:
You're supporting your ventures on amazingly new innovation. Nobody realizes what the genuine worth is…

You likewise should be amazingly cautious about the trades you use. Some are superior to other people – so take care with which one you use.

Be careful about programmers, keep your login subtleties secure and consistently utilize twofold layer confirmation for you.

5. New kid on the block Trading Mistakes To Avoid.

Getting eager. In case you're making great returns, take some of it out in any event! When you're earning substantial sums of money, it's anything but difficult to give eagerness a chance to dominate. In any case, that will just damage you over the long haul…

Never contribute beyond what you can stand to lose. Principle #1 with regards to a contributing. Be dependable and don't go out on a limb.

FUD. FUD = dread, vulnerability and uncertainty. Facebook gatherings are a portion of the most exceedingly terrible for this stuff. Settle on certain choices and stick to them – in light of the fact that nobody comprehends what's on the horizon.

FOMO. Seen an altcoin that is hopped 1,000% in a day? Kindly don't pursue it! The dread of passing up a major opportunity can transform any prepared genius into a credulous new kid on the block. Rather, sit tight for the following open door as opposed to pursuing soaked purchases.

Siphon and dumps. In case you're new to the game, a siphon and dump is the point at which the cost of an altcoin is expanded by a gathering of merchants. It's essentially a trick that you can leave you holding low quality coins. On the off chance that you need assistance recognizing a siphon and dump, read this.

Imbecilic cash. Many low quality altcoins are flooding the market at the present time, and that is just going to deteriorate in 2018. So be cautious who you contribute with and consistently do your own examination.

Set stop misfortunes. With regards to altcoin exchanging, the market can crash really damn rapidly. So ensure your increases and set stop-misfortunes – these will sell your altcoins naturally if they drop by a sensational rate.

Try not to freeze. While exchanging altcoins, I've made $1,000 in my rest – however I've additionally lost comparative sums.

Best Crypto Currency Exchanegs for AltCoins to Buy/Sell Crypto Assets

Gradually and relentlessly, Bitcoin and altcoins are getting consideration from more speculators all around the globe.

What's more, why not? These digital forms of money are on numerous occasions demonstrating themselves to be a place of refuge against the administration's inflationary strategies.

That is the reason a few people are in any event, winning enthusiasm on crypto, while some are doing unadulterated hypothesis with momentary exchanging (for example purchase low, sell high).

What's more, we should not disregard the individuals who are simply beginning by glancing around to discover the response to questions like:

• Where do I purchase such monetary forms?
• What are the best digital currency trades?

In any case, before we talk about the best trades out there, I have to reveal to you that it's not very late to get put resources into cryptographic forms of money. At the hour of this composition, the Bitcoin and altcoin market is at an untouched high, with a market top of $219 billion. I accept we will cross the $300 billion imprint not long from now.

So since you realize you ought to contribute, here's the place you have to go to do that.

Note: This rundown is beginning from simple to utilize trades and moving towards a portion of the propelled trades.

8 Best Cryptocurrency Exchanges for Trading Cryptocurrency

1. Coinbase

Coinbase is a U.S. based crypto trade that serves the worldwide crowd. They are apprentice inviting and offers incredible speed and dependability.

Utilizing CoinBase you can rapidly purchase cryptographic forms of money and exchange simultaneously. They have an application for the two iOS and Android, which gives you the solace of trading digital forms of money from anyplace.

The security standard of CoinBase is truly elevated and they have been around for a long time. CoinBase is upheld in practically all the mainland (Africa, Asia Australia, Europe, North America, South America)

Coinbase likewise underpins well known stable coins, for example, DAI, USDC which is a significant part of any mainstream digital money trade.

2: Binance

Binance is a quickly developing trade that closed its ICO on 21st July 2017 and raised 15,000,000 USD. The organization is enlisted in Malta which is the crypto paradise and offers a blasting quick trade.

Since its ICO to till date, it has developed hugely and is currently put in top 10 digital money trades on the planet. It currently has more than 190 altcoins recorded on it which are just expanding as the days are passing.

Binance being a brought together trade has taken a one of a kind take to extend its business and furthermore gives a fair rebate to informal investors on the off chance that they use BNB coins. BNB is Binance Coin which is the local cash of this stage.

Peruse: Binance Review: Features, Fees in 2019 (Beginner's Guide)

Binance's charge structure is likewise one of a kind. To begin with they have 0.1% standard exchanging charge which is as of now very not exactly different friends. You can even decrease your charge further on the off chance that you pay your exchanging expense BNB as indicated by the underneath demonstrated structure.

To begin with Binance you have to enroll utilizing your email ID and the procedure is very basic and quick. Binance is one of only a handful couple of trades that offers versatile application for iOS and Android.

Being utilizing it for some time, I see it as too simple to even think about trading digital money while moving. You can watch this video to figure out how to utilize their versatile application.

They likewise have forceful plans like multi-lingual help, versatile applications for the two iOS and Android clients, Binance Angel Program, and the Community Coin Per Month and so forth for more reception of their foundation.

Make a record on Binance (Instant enactment) If you want to create Trade on Binance then click on this link to register in Binance:- https://www.binance.com/en/markets? ref=35230773

3: BITMEX

BitMex is high volume crypto trade made by a gifted group of financial specialists, high-recurrence dealers and web designers for the crypto network.

Here you will never discover any issues with respect to the liquidity of your cryptographic forms of money.

The essential cash exchanged on this trade is Bitcoin and its future agreements.

Aside from Bitcoin contracts, one can likewise play around with future agreements for altcoins, for example, Bitcoin Cash, Ethereum, Cardano, Litecoin, Ripple.

The enrollment procedure on BitMex is very basic where you simply need to enlist through your email ID and their expense structure is additionally very direct as demonstrated as follows:

4: KuCoin

KuCoin is another simple and bother free cryptographic money trade. KuCoin offers numerous famous and one of a kind coin, for example, DragonChain, $KCS, and numerous others. Much the same as Binance, they offer a completely utilitarian portable application for Android and iOS.

To begin with KuCoin, you can store any crypto of your decision ex: BTC and start exchanging.

5:Changelly

Changelly is perhaps the most effortless approaches to get tightly to different cryptographic forms of money.

Changelly has a demonstrated reputation of reliably great items being put out into the crypto-space.

Perhaps the best thing about Changelly is that you don't have to experience any long confirmation or enlistment process. You simply sign in with your email ID (or any email ID) and start trading!

At present, it underpins in excess of 35 cryptographic forms of money alongside fiat matches, for example, USD/EUR. It is truly outstanding and most effortless to utilize trades out there. On the off chance that you need to know more, look at Harsh's audit on Changelly.

At the point when you use Changelly to trade digital money, Changelly bots associate continuously to probably the best and busiest cryptographic money trades in the market to get you the best cost.

More often than not, when utilizing Changelly, a crypto-to-crypto trade takes 5 to 30 minutes.

They charge a commission expense of 0.5% on each exchange, which I believe is negligible in return for the unpredictability and hazard that they bear in the interest of their clients. Notwithstanding the commission, an excavator's charge is additionally paid by the client and is deducted legitimately from their crypto balance.

Be that as it may, all you need so as to purchase from Changelly is a VISA/MasterCard (credit/charge card) or any Changelly-upheld cryptographic money and a wallet where you need to get your new coins.

The methodology is straightforward.

Head toward Changelly, and pursue the means given in this guide.

Note: Though this guide tells the best way to purchase Ripple in return for BTC, the procedure is actually the equivalent to purchase some other Changelly-bolstered digital currency.

Also, in the event that you need to purchase cryptos utilizing a VISA/MasterCard, at that point here is their official bit by bit control on doing that. (Despite the fact that this guide is for purchasing BTC utilizing a VISA/MasterCard, the procedure is equivalent to purchasing some other Changelly-bolstered digital money.)

6: HOUBI

Huobi Pro is a universal digital money trade that began in China however now has moved over the world to serve a most extreme number of speculators. It is based out of Singapore and has been working in this space effectively throughout the previous five years.

At this very moment, it involves the #3 spot on CoinMarketCap's rundown of trades by volume and has 244 cryptographic money sets. Subsequently, obviously, of this, you will never confront liquidity issues on this trade.

They additionally have versatile applications for both Android and iOS for clients who need to exchange cryptos in a hurry.

Their enrollment procedure is additionally quite basic and direct, so feel free to do the needful. Gracious, and to make sure you know, the trade expense is likewise truly low. Have a great time.

Do peruse, Huobi Exchange Review and Benefits of HT token: Can It Pull Off Another Binance?

7: BITTREX

Bittrex is a US-based cryptographic money trade that gives you the choice to exchange in excess of 190 digital currencies one after another. They are well-managed and agreeable with the majority of the present US rules, so crypto clients need not stress over the security of their assets.

Bittrex handles one of the biggest BTC exchanging volumes out of the considerable number of trades on the planet.

Here, the clients (purchasers/merchants) choose the rates wherein they need to exchange, and Bittrex charges them a little assistance expense for giving this stage (0.25%).

To begin with Bittrex, you have to enlist and sign in through your email ID, however to pull back assets, you have to do a KYC by presenting your ID archives and telephone number, just as empowering two-factor verification for higher cutoff points.

In any case, one beneficial thing about Bittrex is the record confirmation happens very quick.

Bittrex bolsters two sorts of records:

• Basic Account – withdrawal subsidizes worth up to 3 BTC/day.

• Advanced Account – withdrawal supports worth up to 100 BTC/day.

Bittrex is a "crypto-just" trade, which means it doesn't enable you to store fiat monetary forms, for example, USD, EUR, GBP, and so on.

They give access to cutting edge exchanging apparatuses like candle graphs and focus, however the UI is very perfect and instinctive, so amateurs ought to have no issues.

8: Poloniex

Established by Tristan D'Agosta, Poloniex has been operational since January 2014 and is without a doubt one of the greatest cryptographic money trades on the planet.

It is based out of the United States and offers +100 digital currencies to its clients to exchange.

At the point when you talk about exchange volumes, nothing beats Poloniex. In 2017, Poloniex had the most noteworthy volume for ETH in light of the fact that it underpins an autonomous Ethereum showcase just as a BTC advertise.

It is a crypto-just trade, however you can begin exchanging effectively by keeping USDT (Tether dollars).

Poloniex additionally has zoomable candle diagrams for 5-minutes, 15-minutes, 30-minutes, 2-hours, 4-hours, and 1-day, alongside a stop-limit highlight for cutting edge digital money dealers.

Poloniex charges an expense of 0.15% to 0.25% on all exchanges relying on whether you are a creator or a taker.

So on the off chance that you are hoping to exchange an assortment of altcoins, at that point you should give Poloniex a shot.

To begin with Poloniex, pursue this official guide.

Keep in mind: As soon as you pursue Poloniex utilizing your email, do try to empower two-factor verification!

Conclusion:

As you make all the way here reading & learning new ways all about to make money from home that is to Utilize your skills and expertise into the work you want to do, the most experience you have in specific work field.

We learned about Graphic Designing and from that we can pick Logo Design as a Most Trending work field that is never going to end ever and along with that having Photoshop skills you can do some good graphic Designing too.

Web Development requires expert people for some big Projects and newbies can also take a part in that work to prove their skills Front end Development is all about

Themes and Website Design. So, if you do learn some of these skills you can make some pretty amount on Freelancing platforms,

If you don't have time to Learn skills right now, then you can move forward with the Simple Work Done jobs as a Virtual Assistant and Data Entry Jobs that requires good grip on your work focus in order to Get Done with the Client.

And last but not the least, we discuss about Trading online which includes Bitcoin, Forex Trading. You must invest some money and then Learn some risk management ways to start trading online so that you don't take a loss on your portfolio.
Bitcoin is just like a Digital Gold and it is becoming famous rapidly, so take your chances and Dive Deep into the Skill that suits you the Most.

Thank You for Reading this Book, hope this might get you the Right Success Path.

GOOD LUCK